"I was just given a copy of your book. Believe me, I am having trouble _____ work done because I just want to sit and read it. It is hard to put down!"

CLARISSE MAXWELL, Idaho Black History Museum, Boise ID

"This greater-than-life work, created out of purity of motive, will surely aid all of us dedicated to dismantling racism."

CHERRY STEINWENDER, Center for the Healing of Racism, Houston TX

"I find it comforting and validating to browse through the quotes at times when spirits are low!"

DOUGLAS C. REYNOLDS, Belmont Against Racism, Belmont MA

"It is kind of like a bible to me. I pick it up and browse it daily. It reinforces things I know and puts perspective and knowledge from so many people I respect at my fingertips."

SHARON LA CHAPPELLE, Racial Justice Institute, Grand Rapids, MI

"Everyone who reads this book will learn something about himself or herself. It definitely is an eye opener."

VERNITA WILLIAMS, Defense Logistics Agency, Battle Creek MI

"The quotations raise 'gut-wrenching' questions involved in dealing with the disease of racism rather than just the symptoms."

WM. J. ARTHUR, Leadership Morality Institute, Columbus GA

"One is not quite the same person when one has finished reading it that one was before."

JEAN ALBAUM, Senior Adjunct Professor, University of La Verne, La Verne CA

"Your book is meaningfully on target. Thank you for sharing your vision, your books, and your heart."

JAN E. GILLESPIE, Samuel L. Fels Cluster, The School District of Philadelphia PA

"The book is a penetrating reminder of how far America has come, and how far we must go in this minefield of racial interplay. You have done a superb job!"

PAUL BAYLESS, Affirmative Action Office, Indiana U/Purdue U, Indianapolis IN

"I cannot imagine anyone involved in social justice or the work of extending understanding and respect among all people not having this enriching collection."

LAURA A. D'ALISERA, National Conference for Community and Justice, Jacksonville FL

"We are delighted to have access to a book that is as enlightening as it is truthful."
JUDITH C. AMBER, Episcopal Diocese of Nebraska, Lincoln NE

"It will have a lasting effect wherever it lands. Congratulations on a job well done."
TERRY E. HESS, Regional Initiative for Diversity Education, St. Cloud MN

"Your book has been a marvelous supplement to our efforts in understanding racial differences among people and appreciating diversity within our society."
DR. MAYNARD M. SUFFREDINI, JR., Principal, Burlington High School, Burlington MA

"It will surely help toward the long overdue victory over racism in our country."
JAMES B. FAILS, Citizens Upholding Racial Equality, Fremont OH

"Your amazing book is doing wonderful work in raising the consciousness of all who open it."
CONNIE STERNBERG, Unitarian Universalist Society: East, Manchester CT

"Wide-ranging and thought-provoking, this book grapples with one of America's most troubling, historically persistent, and important issues."
JEFF LOWENSTEIN, Facing History and Ourselves, Boston MA

"Your book is very powerful and moving. It will have a great, inspirational impact."
WILLIAM A. HOWE, Connecticut State Department of Education, Hartford CT

"Thank you for providing such an easy and innovative way for talking about this most sensitive topic." VICKY B. PARTIN, Chattahoochee Valley Episcopal Miinistry, Columbus GA

"This book expresses in the deepest sense the fundamental rights guaranteed to 'We, the People' by the Constitution of the United States. It should be read and studied by each and every one of us."
ARTHUR KINOY, Professor Emeritus of Constitutional Law, Rutgers University Law School, NJ

"The book is a treasure of reference as America struggles with what appears to be her terminal illness." REV. LOUIS A. CHASE, Hamilton United Methodist Church, Los Angeles CA

"The mixture of quotes in this wonderful book creates an enlightening and thought-challenging work."
CONNIE BENJAMIN, YWCA, Lincoln NE

"Racism teaches hard lessons, but this book will help you laugh while you learn. We find it indispensable. . . . a pithy work that makes for very good reading."
RUBY DEE AND OSSIE DAVIS, Actors / activists

"This unique collection is a gem of great value. Every teacher, preacher, parent, public servant — indeed, every American — should have a copy."
REV. LUCIUS WALKER, JR., The Interreligious Foundation for Community Organization, New York NY

"Your book is remarkable in that it makes us think where we came from, where we are, and where we are headed."
FRANCES O. ELLINGBERG, New Hope Baptist Church, Oakland CA

"There is so much in the variety and substance of the quotes that is inspirational, thought provoking and challenging — a job well done!"
REGELYN W. EDWARDS, Racial Conciliation Outreach, Building Together Ministries, Raleigh NC

"The book is marvelous in its conception and execution. You have made a remarkable contribution to human understanding."
MOLEFI KETE ASANTE, Professor, African-American Studies, Temple University, Philadelphia PA

"The voices of dignity, enlightenment, poetry, and rage assembled in this masterfully edited volume will inspire readers of all ages to look freshly on the world we inhabit, and to keep working to make it better."
HAMILTON FISH, Nation Institute, New York NY

"Congratulations on producing a really worthwhile effort. The ground covered, the way the material is arranged, the movement from section to section, the choice of quotes and illustrations, all work wonderfully well. A superb job!"
NANCY MURRAY, The Bill of Rights Education Project, ACLU, Boston MA

"Your book is an example of what one of my divinity school professors called 'ripple ethics' — a single effort which creates an ever-widening response."
JUDITH B. BRAIN, Pastor, Pilgrim Congregational Church, UCC, Lexington MA

"In this rich anthology of affirmations, assertions, definitions, analyses, and assessments of race and racism one comes as close as is possible to understanding what it is like to be in someone else's skin in America."
JOEL COLTON, Professor Emeritus of History, Duke University, Durham NC

"What a powerful start to a new millennium! All of us need its wisdom and courage." ANN DUCKLESS, Student Assistance Coordinator, Hollis/Brookline Schools, Hollis NH

"May the book be absorbed for generations to come and its contents deeply treasured." SISTER MARY DOOLEY, Mother Caroline Academy & Education Center, Dorchester MA

"And don't call *me* a racist!"

**A treasury of quotes
on the past, present, and future
of the color line in America**

SELECTED AND ARRANGED BY Ella Mazel

ARGONAUT PRESS / LEXINGTON, MASSACHUSETTS

The cartoons on pages 44 and 128, © 1994, have been generously contributed
by Kirk Anderson, e-mail: kirka@pioneerplanet.infi.net

The right to reproduce *Best Buddies* [page 130] has been generously contributed
by The Estate of Keith Haring

Lyric excerpt [page 95] from "Ballad for Americans" by John Latouche and Earl Robinson
© 1939, 1940 (Copyrights Renewed) EMI Robbins Catalog Inc.
All Rights Reserved   Used by Permission
WARNER BROS. PUBLICATIONS U.S. INC., Miami, FL 33014

Lyric excerpts [page 130] of "You've Got To Be Carefully Taught" by Richard Rodgers and Oscar Hammerstein II
Copyright © 1949 by Richard Rodgers and Oscar Hammerstein II
Copyright Renewed WILLIAMSON MUSIC owner of publication and allied rights throughout the world
International Copyright Secured   Reprinted by Permission   All Rights Reserved

EIGHTH PRINTING

Library of Congress Catalog Card Number 98-74108

Dedication

To **Booker T. Washington,**
from whose autobiography, UP FROM SLAVERY, which I read as a child in the 1920s,
I learned the meaning of *empathy*.

To **Paul Robeson,**
from whose lifelong struggle on behalf of his people
and of working people around the world
I learned the meaning of the word *hero*.

To **Dean Dixon,**
from whose frustration over being denied permanent conductorship
of a major orchestra in the United States because of his color
I learned the meaning of *black rage*.

To the **Joint Veterans' Council of Peekskill, New York,**
from whose instigation of mob violence
to prevent a concert by Paul Robeson (the first of the two 1949 "riots")
I learned firsthand the meaning of the *fear* for one's life
that accompanies ugly hatred, racial insults, and physical attack.

To **Zola G.**,
the hard-working young black single mother
from whose sharing of her history and her dreams
I learned the importance of the *dignity*
without which she "would slowly and surely die."

To **Eddie Vanderlip,**
from whose completion of high school (and later, junior college)
after I had tutored him in algebra and self-esteem
I learned that it was possible to *make a difference* in one person's life.

To **Dick M.**,
from whose angry recital of clichés about blacks today
and the disclaimer that followed (which inspired, and became the title of, this book)
I learned that *"nice" white people can be racist* even when they think they're not.

Contents

[CONTINUED]

From me to you

Most of us white folk go through life comfortably without being conscious of the innumerable ways in which we are automatically privileged by the luck of our racial draw. This may not make us "racists" — but it makes us, unwittingly, beneficiaries of racism.

Bernice Albertine King writes of her father's magnificent "I Have a Dream" speech that its "effect was to comfort the disturbed, but not without disturbing the comfortable."

It's primarily to "disturb the comfortable" that I've assembled in this book a progression of quotes that convey — in the voices of both blacks and whites — the history, the perceptions, the psychic scars, and the despair, that underlie the racial breach in the United States today. Out of the pain, finally, comes the hope for healing, which seems the only option if the country is to progress, let alone survive.

Why the focus on white/black racism?

Most manifestations of prejudice and racism affect not only African-Americans but Native Americans, Asian-Americans, Latinos, and other "people of color." These minorities, too, experience discrimination in housing, education, and employment. They, too, are subjected daily to humiliation or worse.

Still, by the time you've finished this book, I hope you will understand why:

- Christopher Edley, Jr., says that: "The black-white tension is the heart, the principal generator of the minority-rights controversy in national policy argument and in most areas of the country."
- Patricia Williams wonders: "How can it be that so many well-meaning white people have never thought about race when so few blacks pass a single day without being reminded of it?"
- Andrew Young needs to point out that: "Most White Americans don't even know the history of slavery and the long continuing struggle of blacks to overcome it."
- Martin Luther King, Jr., tells how: "Instinctively we struck out for dignity first because personal degradation as an inferior human being was even more keenly felt than material privation."
- Shirley Chisholm cries out in frustration: "My God, what do we want? What does any human being want?"

Whose voices do we hear?

You will find here the words of writers and speakers ranging from apologists for slavery in the mid-1800s to former slaves like Frederick Douglass and Booker T. Washington at the end of the century; from W.E.B. Du Bois in the early 1900s to President Clinton and Oprah Winfrey as we near the millennium.

Listen to firebrands like Stokeley Carmichael and Malcolm X alongside the bitter but ultimately hopeful Arthur Ashe and the soft-spoken Muhammad Ali.

Discover, as I did, the brilliance of the *written* words of Martin Luther King, Jr.; the explosive eloquence of Lerone Bennett, Jr., and Randall Robinson; the humor of Langston Hughes and the Delany sisters; the up-front denunciations of racism by Colin Powell; the frankness of Harlon L. Dalton and Clarence Page; the revelations by Lillian Smith and Sarah Patton Boyle of what it meant to grow up white in the South.

Familiar names like Maya Angelou and Toni Morrison, Harry Belafonte and Sammy Davis, Jr., mingle with those of the man and woman in the street whose wise insights are captured in interviews by Studs Terkel — plus those of a lot of other "ordinary" people and lesser-known writers.

The prose of such current intellectual activists as Cornel West, Henry Louis Gates, Jr., and Orlando Patterson appears side by side with that of Gordon Allport in the seminal *The Nature of Prejudice* and Gunnar Myrdal in his classic, *The American Dilemma*.

You will find the views of pessimists and optimists, with their expressions of despair and of hope; of radicals and conservatives, with their conflicting approaches on integration versus separation or affirmative action versus so-called "preferences" — with both blacks and whites on opposite sides of each issue.

There are some topics I have avoided almost entirely because they are so historically divisive that they would sidetrack the central ideas in this book, as they have in life — the matter of intermarriage, for example, on which there are as strong differences of opinion in the black as in the white "community" — ranging from those who see "assimilation" as a utopian ideal to those who perceive it as genocide.

Where do the quotes come from?

As Andrew Hacker points out, "No one could possibly tally all the books and articles that have been written about race in America," and the sheer volume of available material is indeed overwhelming. So I drew the line when I had worked my way through a more-or-less random, but representative, number of books that include biographies and autobiographies, collections of essays by individual writers, anthologies, sociological studies, and histories.

In addition, many of the quotes come from the newspaper I read every morning — there's hardly a day without at least one article relating to race. Others are from magazines, like *Newsweek* and *Ebony*. Then there's the Internet, from which I have downloaded all of the press releases from the White House on the President's Race Initiative. On the Web I also found some fascinating material ranging from a book published by a former slave to a southern separatist movement of today.

All in all, I hope my research into the many facets of racism will provide food for thought for you as an individual, and encourage you to explore in more detail the writings of some of the authors I have quoted. Moreover, the book can serve both as a starting point for group discussions and as an educational resource for schools, libraries, and outreach programs.

Can anything be done?

We may not be able to solve the deeply entrenched social and economic problems that beset so many Americans, but each of us can "be more than passively good-hearted," as Langston Hughes suggests, "try equality on for size," as Harlon Dalton proposes, and become "antiracist," as Clarence Page urges.

At the very least — by enlarging what Dr. King called our "capacity to empathize," and practicing "the good old Golden Rule," as Orlando Patterson recommends — perhaps each of us *can* make a difference.

PLEASE NOTE THE LISTINGS STARTING ON PAGE 148

For the **book, article, or speech** from which a quote is excerpted, and for **other quotes** by the same person, see INDEX/SOURCES. For information about **the person** quoted, see THE VOICES. For information about a **person mentioned** in a quote, see ABOUT PEOPLE.

"And don't call *me* a racist!"

I suppose it was naive of me to think
. . . that if one only searched one's heart
one would know
that none of us is responsible
for the complexion of his skin,
and that we could not change it if we wished to,
and many of us don't wish to,
and that this fact of nature
offers no clue to the character or quality
of the person underneath.

MARIAN ANDERSON, 1956

THE RACIAL DIVIDE

The "American Dilemma"
. . . is the ever-raging conflict between,
on the one hand,
the valuations preserved on the general plane
which we shall call the "American Creed,"
where the American thinks, talks, and acts
under the influence
of high national and Christian precepts,
and, on the other hand,
the valuations on specific planes
of individual and group living,
where personal and local interests
. . . and all sorts of miscellaneous wants,
impulses, and habits dominate his outlook.

GUNNAR MYRDAL, 1942

Race is the least reliable information you can have
about someone. It's real information,
but it tells you next to nothing.
TONI MORRISON, 1998

My son came to me one day and asked how I'd feel
if he married a white woman. I told him that
love doesn't have a color.
NORMA STEVENSON, 1992

Isn't love more important than color?
JAMES BALDWIN, 1963

There is no color line in death.
LANGSTON HUGHES, 1945

Past / Present / Future

America is false to the past, false to the present, and solemnly binds herself to be false to the future.
FREDERICK DOUGLASS, 1852

Prejudice is a burden which confuses the past, threatens the future, and renders the present inaccessible.
MAYA ANGELOU, 1986

There is never time in the future in which we will work out our salvation. The challenge is in the moment, the time is always now.
JAMES BALDWIN, 1961

To those Arkansans who ask how long the state will have to deal with the legacy of Little Rock: Until justice is the same for every human being, whether he or she is black or white, we will deal with it. Until the same rules apply to get a bank loan for every person regardless of who he or she is, we will deal with it. As long as there are whites who turn around and see a black person coming and it brings fear to their hearts, we'll deal with it. And as long as there are blacks who have resentment toward a white person, we'll deal with it.
GOVERNOR MIKE HUCKABEE, 1997

The specter of color is apparent even when it goes unmentioned, and it is all too often the unseen force that influences public policy as well as private relationships. There is nothing more remarkable than the ingenuity that the various demarcations of the color line reflect. If only the same creative energy could be used to eradicate the color line; then its days would indeed be numbered.
JOHN HOPE FRANKLIN, 1993

At this time when there is more cause for hope than fear, when we are not driven by some emergency or some imminent cataclysm in our society, we really have not only an opportunity but an obligation to address and to better resolve the vexing, perplexing, often painful issues surrounding our racial history and future.
PRESIDENT BILL CLINTON, (July 17) 1997

The age-old racial divide is no less yawning than before.
RANDALL ROBINSON, 1998

5

At least at the level of surveys, real progress has taken place in the degree to which white Americans have accepted ideals of racial justice and integration that, before the Civil Rights Act of 1964, were considered . . . in some parts of the country, dangerous and subversive. If words were all that mattered, America would be far along toward full repudiation of its racist past.   ALAN WOLFE, 1998

Now we hear voices in America arguing that Dr. King's struggle is over — that we've reached the promised land. Maybe they're just carried away by the arrival of the Millennium, and are deluding themselves that when the calendar turns to the year 2000, human beings will have been perfected.   VICE PRESIDENT AL GORE, 1998

I almost weep when I see what has happened to the civil rights movement, the bloody struggles for racial justice . . . . So much that was won over the bites of police dogs, the truncheons of bigoted cops, has been diluted — or lost.   CARL T. ROWAN, 1991

I feel such heavy sadness that my children . . . will continue to be caught in the vise of this venomous, perverse attitudinal phenomenon that too many in our society intentionally and unintentionally perpetuate.
JEAN TUCKER MANN, 1997

A suffering people has the capacity to develop long patience and endurance, and to look on the fact of blackness as a cross to bear. And we bear it quite well. But my fear is that in this generation we have been unable to transmit to our young people the need to bear crosses.
CHARLES H. KING, JR., 1983

Well-funded pressure groups and opinion-makers insist that "racism is over" and that even in its heyday, it wasn't so bad. They are rewriting history to reflect their views.
PROJECT HIP-HOP, 1997

We must delve into the depths where neither liberals nor conservatives dare to tread, namely, into the murky waters of despair and dread that now flood the streets of black America.
CORNEL WEST, 1993

Americans couldn't answer the basic questions about race in 1839 and it led to war. We can't answer them fully today, but it's still too soon and too important to stop trying.
JONATHAN ALTER, 1997

Discrimination is not just an ugly stain from this nation's past, it's still the reality of the present.
ANDREW CUOMO, 1998

For better / For worse

The ideals that bind us together are as old as our nation, but so are the forces that pull us apart.
PRESIDENT BILL CLINTON
(June 14) 1997

Most white people seem to think we've come further than most black people think we have. The twin goals of achieving racial equality and the elimination of racial prejudice continue to recede before all the advances that we have made.
WILLIAM F. WINTER, 1997

To suggest that the problem of the twenty-first century will be the problem of the color line is not to ignore the changes that have occurred in this as well as in other centuries. It is merely to take notice of the obvious fact that the changes have not been sufficient to eliminate the color line as a problem, arguably the most tragic and persistent social problem of the nation's history.
JOHN HOPE FRANKLIN, 1993

Though Americans prefer to dwell on parables of white virtue and black advancement — culminating in the flowering of good will all around — events periodically force us to widen our gaze and to focus on terrain we would rather not see.
ELLIS COSE, 1997

Thanks to the sixties, we have a new climate of race relations in the country. Black mayors in our largest cities. Corporate executives. On the other hand, we have Depression levels of unemployment, the collapse of the public school system, and the epidemic of hard drugs. Everything appears to have changed, yet nothing has changed. Black people are still at the bottom.
LERONE BENNETT, JR., 1992

There are so many things better for black Americans than ever before, with the promise of more, but these signs are counterbalanced by the signs of no progress in some quarters and even backward motion in others.
ANTHONY WALTON, 1993

Things are getting better. Things have gotten better. Things are getting worse at the same time.
DAVID SHIPLER, 1997

7

African-Americans, perhaps still placated by the fool's gold of integration as an endgame achievement, seem not to have noticed our worsening condition with any alarm. At some point beyond the peak of the civil rights movement, we lost our bearings, as if sleepwalking. . . . Our longitude had changed but our latitude was virtually the same.

Most blacks seem to agree that the quality of our lives is worse now than ten years ago. It is almost certainly worse than in the 1960s.   ARTHUR ASHE, 1993

In many ways, the black community's current crisis is more vexing, if less painful, than that presented by segregation forty years ago. We were united then, if only in what we were against. Now, with legal segregation abolished, we are without benefit of even that loathsome but unifying condition.   RANDALL ROBINSON, 1998

The more settled race relations seem to be, the more likely they are raging beneath the surface.

A two-tiered universe of perception rotates around an axis defined by race. While good fortune lights one side, despair darkens the other. It is rarely sunny at the same time in white and black America.
    MICHAEL ERIC DYSON, 1996

The masses of our people recognize that most of the defining issues of the Civil Rights Movement *no longer exist*. We face an unprecedented crisis of poverty, violence, joblessness, and social despair, and the old approaches are no longer sufficient or viable.
    MANNING MARABLE, 1997

The story about race in America over the past two or three decades is a complicated one. Some black Americans are doing better than ever; others worse than ever. Integration and segregation seem to be increasing at the same time. Compared with where we were, there is progress. Compared with where we should be, that progress is insufficient.   ALAN WOLFE, 1998

At one time I thought things were getting better. I really did. I look back, the past years seems like we're backsliding, all the way backwards. It seems like everybody hates everybody.   JULIAN JEFFERSON, 1992

We have everything we fought for, yet we still don't have what we need.
JESSE JACKSON, 1998

Racism is alive and well in America, shaping our suburban geography and weaving through our private conversations. . . . While residential segregation decreases for most racial and ethnic groups with additional education, income, and occupational status, this does not hold true for African Americans.

CHARLES R. LAWRENCE III / MARI J. MATSUDA, 1997

It is a good time to be an American. Unrivaled prosperity dominates the land, and many of the ghosts of our past are being confronted with new passion. Yet poverty and despair . . . are also growing with biblical certainty.

KELVIN SHAWN SEALEY, 1997

The racism that made slavery feasible is far from dead in the last decade of twentieth-century America; and the civil rights gains, so hard won, are being steadily eroded. . . . Even the most successful of us are haunted by the plight of our less fortunate brethren who . . . live beyond the pale of the American Dream.   DERRICK BELL, 1992

Young people these days . . . want to keep it real. And keeping it real means, in fact, understanding that the white supremacy you thought you could push back permeates every nook and cranny of this nation so deeply that you ought to wake up and recognize how deep it is.

HARRY BELAFONTE, 1997

Racist behavior has declined, but racist attitudes have not.
CLYDE W. FORD, **1994**

Prejudice is . . .

Moss-covered opinions assume the disproportioned form of prejudices when they are indolently adopted only because age has given them a venerable aspect, though the reason on which they were built ceases to be a reason, or cannot be traced.   MARY WOLLSTONECRAFT, 1792

A deeply held prejudice will actually cause our senses to accommodate to the prejudice rather than to the reality of what they are seeing or hearing.
                                JOHN HOWARD GRIFFIN, 1977

Even prejudice cannot be stereotyped, because no single theory can encompass the complex, deeply interrelated, and often subtle influences that combine to make all human personalities.   SARA BULLARD, 1996

We may lay it down as a general law applying to all social phenomena that *multiple causation* is invariably at work and nowhere is the law more clearly applicable than to prejudice.   GORDON ALLPORT, 1954

Prejudice is not automatically and immediately eliminated by changes in social institutions. . . . People cling to ideas and behavior that are clearly not only in conflict with reality and developing knowledge, but are also destructive to themselves.
                                ALEXANDER THOMAS, M.D., 1972

Prejudice, n. A vagrant opinion without visible means of support.
                AMBROSE BIERCE, 1906

Men, in general, seem to employ their reason to justify prejudices . . . rather than to root them out.
        MARY WOLLSTONECRAFT, 1792

Prejudgments become prejudices only if they are not reversible when exposed to new knowledge.
        GORDON ALLPORT, 1954

One reason why prejudice, though earning its bad name, so often fails even to be arrested is its genuinely being so evasive of definition.
        CHRISTOPHER RICKS, 1988

People who are aware of, and ashamed of, their prejudices are well on the road to eliminating them.
GORDON ALLPORT, 1954

When a particular kind of prejudice runs very deep, sometimes it can seem as though the prejudice has always existed and will always exist, as though it were as much a fact of life as people's need to eat or to shelter themselves.   RACHEL KRANZ, 1992

Prejudice is a shape shifter. It's very agile in taking forms that seem acceptable on the surface.
DAVID SHIPLER, 1997

We can at least *try* to understand our own motives, passions, and prejudices, so as to be conscious of what we are doing when we appeal to those of others. This is very difficult, because our own prejudice and emotional bias always seem to us so rational.   T. S. ELIOT, 1950

Every person who quietly goes along with or benefits from prejudice is responsible for that prejudice.

Prejudice comes from being in the dark; sunlight disinfects it.

A society struggles to fulfill its best instincts, even as an individual does, and generally makes just as hard going of it. The fight against prejudice is an inevitable process. Man has been warring against his own lower nature ever since he found out he had one, and the battle against intolerance is part of the same old struggle between good and evil that has preoccupied us ever since we gave up swinging from trees.   MARGARET HALSEY, 1946

It would be nice if we could simply vacuum the prejudice from people's minds, but life isn't that simple.

Being on the receiving end of prejudice spawns more prejudice.
MUHAMMAD ALI, 1996

Is there less prejudice today? It is certainly less obvious, and what remains of it is mostly denied. . . . the phrase "I'm not prejudiced" . . . is inevitably followed by a qualifier — "I'm not prejudiced, but . . . "
CLARENCE PAGE, 1996

I don't think the problem is insoluble. I'm not an optimist, but I have a lot of hope. People change. . . . That's why we shouldn't live forever. . . A new generation may not have the experiences and prejudices of the older.
BILL HOHRI, 1992

We cannot choose the color of our skin, but we can choose the nature of our beliefs.
CLYDE W. FORD, 1994

Prejudice is learned. It's not a self-winding watch.

MUHAMMAD ALI, 1996

Many people give the appearance of progress by shedding the prejudices and irrational postulates of one generation only to acquire those of the next.

T. S. ELIOT, 1937

Most of us are no more guilty of acquiring our prejudices than we are guilty of acquiring a disfiguring pockmark from some childhood illness.

JOHN HOWARD GRIFFIN, 1977

No child is born prejudiced. His prejudices are always acquired . . . chiefly in fulfillment of his own needs. Yet the context of his learning is always the social structure in which his personality develops.

GORDON ALLPORT, 1954

Social scientists are now convinced that children learn social, racial, and religious prejudices in the course of observing, and being influenced by, the existence of patterns in the culture in which they live.

KENNETH B. CLARK, 1963

One doesn't decide on bigotry or altruism the way one chooses a college major. The twig is bent early and keeps its shape throughout. There are of course exceptions, but I suspect, without benefit of survey data, that they are few.

RANDALL ROBINSON, 1998

Working with children is the easiest part of educating for democracy, because children are still undefeated and have no stake in being prejudiced.

MARGARET HALSEY, 1946

Adults should bite their tongues before passing on old prejudices.
HILLARY CLINTON, 1997

Racism is . . .

Racism is . . . a negation of the deepest identity of the human being, who is a person created in the image and likeness of God.
POPE JOHN PAUL, 1997

Competing definitions of the R-word illuminate the boundaries of America's racial divide as brightly as landing lights on the landscape at night.

Many demand that we "get past race." But denials of a cancer, no matter how vigorous they may be, will not make the malignancy go away.
CLARENCE PAGE, 1996

Racism is a reflection of personal and collective anxieties lodged deep in the hearts and minds of white Americans.
LERONE BENNETT, JR., 1965

Racism . . . is not simply about the attitudes, dislikes and motivation of individuals or individual acts of bigotry and discrimination. Instead, racism refers to the way society as a whole is arranged, and how the economic, educational, cultural and social rewards of that society are distributed. It is about collective injustice.
PROJECT HIP-HOP, 1997

Something called racism obviously exists. . . . an incubus that has haunted this country since Europeans first set foot on the continent. It goes beyond prejudice and discrimination, and even transcends bigotry, largely because it arises from outlooks and assumptions of which we are largely unaware.
ANDREW HACKER, 1992

Race is for me a more onerous burden than AIDS. My disease is the result of biological factors over which we . . . have had no control. Racism . . . is entirely made by people, and therefore it hurts . . . infinitely more.
ARTHUR ASHE, 1993

Racism is a sensitive word. Americans often avoid mentioning it, even when it is relevant. . . . It is a sensitive word because it exposes so much, institutionally and personally. It is a Rorschach word, a linguistic inkblot test. How you define it reveals something important about you, how you see the world and your place in it.
CLARENCE PAGE, 1996

Racial prejudices are indications of a disturbed and potentially unstable society.
KENNETH B. CLARK, 1963

Americans who would never embrace racism in the specifics of persons and places will express bigotry ruthlessly in generalities.
CARL T. ROWAN, 1991

In our society, racist acts and attitudes are so institutionalized that they can be indulged in as a matter of course by persons who are not pathological.
ALEXANDER THOMAS, M.D. 1972

Most of us remain trapped in the narrow framework of the dominant liberal and conservative views of race in America, which with its worn-out vocabulary leaves us intellectually debilitated, morally disempowered, and personally depressed.
CORNEL WEST, 1993

Blacks have a condition, not a problem. Whites have the problem, racism, that creates our condition. All we can do is react.
C. T. VIVIAN, 1992

I am not antiwhite, because I understand that white people, like black ones, are victims of a racist society. They are products of their time and place.
SHIRLEY CHISHOLM, 1970

Daddy taught me that racism was a sickness and to have compassion for racist whites as I would have compassion for a polio victim. Racism wasn't a problem with me, he told me, it was a problem they had.
ANDREW YOUNG, 1996

Racism, unfortunately, is not the monopoly of a single type of personality structure. All kinds of people can be and are racists: normal and abnormal, paranoid and non-paranoid, aggressive and passive, domineering and submissive.
ALEXANDER THOMAS, M.D., 1972

A candid examination of *race* matters takes us to the core of the crisis of American democracy. And the degree to which race *matters* in the plight and predicament of fellow citizens is a crucial measure of whether we can keep alive the best of this democratic experiment we call America.
CORNEL WEST, 1994

To gloss over race in a racist society may in itself be a capitulation to racism.
ALEXANDER THOMAS, M.D., 1972

. . . prejudice + power

Power concedes nothing without demand. It never did and it never will. Find out just what any people will quietly submit to and you have found out the exact measure of injustice and wrong which will be imposed upon them.
FREDERICK DOUGLASS, 1857

Regardless of form, prejudice backed by power deprives another person of his or her rights.
MUHAMMAD ALI, 1996

Black people have always known, often too well for our own good, in our collectively delimiting racial subconscious, who owns the country and just how closely those owners listen to us.
RANDALL ROBINSON, 1998

Practically all the economic, social, and political power is held by whites. The Negroes do not by far have anything approaching a tenth of the things worth having in America. It is thus the white majority group that naturally determines the Negro's "place." All our attempts to reach scientific explanations of why the Negroes are what they are and why they live as they do have regularly led to determinants on the white side of the race line.
GUNNAR MYRDAL, 1942

Until black people as a whole gain power, it's not a question of where you are geographically if you're black; it's a question of where you are psychologically. No matter where you place black people under present conditions, they'll still be powerless, still subject to the whims and decisions of the white political and economic apparatus.
ELDRIDGE CLEAVER, 1969

Most talk by whites about equal opportunity seems to me now to be about equal opportunity to try to get into a position of dominance while denying that *systems* of dominance exist.
PEGGY MCINTOSH, 1988

My innermost stirrings inevitably have to do with trying to overcome racism and other forms of social injustice, with the search for dignity and power for blacks in a world so often hostile to us.
ARTHUR ASHE, 1993

The only thing white people have that black people need, or should want, is power.
JAMES BALDWIN, 1963

The answer to the problems of black people is in the hands of white society because white institutions hold the power. Blacks are powerless. Period.
CHARLES H. KING, JR., 1983

Until you talk about power and privilege, you can't talk about change. It's hard for white Americans to deal with their own racism.
JOHN TUCKER, 1997

I hate it when people throw around the terms reverse racism. I can be prejudiced but not racist. To be a racist, you have to be able to oppress another race. To do that, you have to have economic and political power. Blacks don't have that; whites do.
DAWN KELLY, 1992

Individuals who do not have power may hold racist views, but they seldom cause much harm. . . . The significance of racism lies in the way it consigns certain human beings to the margins of society, if not painful lives and early deaths. . . . No white person can claim to have suffered in such ways because of ideas that may be held about them by some black citizens.
ANDREW HACKER, 1992

The one thing that various racial classifications adopted by different countries do share is that they evolved over time to serve the interests of those with power. In colonial America . . . white and Black were soon driven far apart, as slaves became property and were written out of the human race.
PROJECT HIP-HOP, 1997

The white man is dead. Men with pale skins still live. But the *idea* of a man with a certain color skin and a mandate from God to order and regulate the lives of men with darker skins: that idea is dead. . . . We no longer live in a world controlled by that idea, though some people, Negroes and whites, have not read the obituary notices.
LERONE BENNETT, JR., 1964

In my version of the Promised Land, I would not eliminate race, but I would eliminate the pecking order to which it is so closely tied. I have no idea what meaning, if any, race would acquire once it was detached from issues of privilege and power. . . . But for now at least, I would be happy to just let it evolve.
HARLON L. DALTON, 1995

Racism is nothing more or less than white privilege, white power, and white violence.
MANNING MARABLE, 1997

. . . prejudice + money

Poverty and Jim Crow are sisters under the skin. To make a decent, happy America, both must go. The sooner the better.
LANGSTON HUGHES, 1948

We now feel more like brothers and sisters than co-workers. We all learned something about color. It comes down to green.
GLORIA HARRIS, 1997
United Parcel striker

To those who believe the battle against discrimination has been won, I say, look at the realities of paychecks and power.
LINDA CHAVEZ-THOMPSON
1997

Many black folk now reside in a jungle ruled by a cut-throat market morality devoid of any faith in deliverance or hope for freedom.
CORNEL WEST, 1993

Both white and black farmers are fleeced by this financial system. But white and black farmers won't combine against a common foe on account of race prejudice. Race antagonism, then, is profitable to those who own the farms, the mills, the railroads and the banks.
A. PHILIP RANDOLPH / CHANDLER OWEN, 1919

Most white people are ignorant of what they have done to the Negro in the economic field. . . . We frankly do not believe that the Negro's economic status would have been nearly so bad if white people realized how all specific economic discriminations add up, and how effectively they bar the way for the Negro when he attempts to better himself.
ARNOLD ROSE, 1948

Racism is not merely exclusion on the basis of race but exclusion for the purpose of subjugating or maintaining subjugation. The goal of the racists is to keep black people on the bottom, arbitrarily and dictatorially, as they have done in this country for over three hundred years.
STOKELY CARMICHAEL / CHARLES V. HAMILTON, 1967

To solve the race problem you're going to have to deal with the poverty problem. And when most whites are dealing with banks and private financial institutions, and a large percentage of blacks are dealing with public assistance, you're going to have different points of view.
D. J. BEATTY, 1997

When morality comes up against profit, it is seldom that profit loses.
SHIRLEY CHISHOLM, 1970

VOICES from *RACE: How Blacks and Whites Think and Feel About the American Obsession* [TERKEL, 1992]

You hear people say Pull yourself up by your bootstraps, and you don't even have shoes. You're barefooted. What are you going to pull yourself up by? Our country owes every citizen . . . a means of livelihood. Not a handout, but a way to make it. 　　　　　MAMIE MOBLEY

If there was enough work for everybody, there wouldn't be so much animosity. We wouldn't have this fear of a black person getting a job, who may not be qualified. I think most black people before they get a job have to be doubly qualified. It's changed a lot, but not much. 　　　PEGGY TERRY

I think the bottom's going to have to fall out and then there won't be any such thing as color. I think that in the 1990s and maybe all the way into the year 2000, the United States is going to go through a tremendous change. I think it has to. The wealth is too imbalanced. . . . We have to clear up a lot of things. 　　　CAROL FREEMAN

The funny thing is I think the gap between white and black is lessening because we are all beginning to see the bigger monster. It's out there trying to devour all people. I left the colored thing and went into class separation. Now it ain't hardly a class separation

no more. It used to be the poor, the middle class, the upper-middle class and the rich. Now it's down to the poor and the rich. The middle class is nothing but putty. To be used. 　　　LITTLE DOVIE THURMAN

I don't think the company is racist. That's too simple. It's the bottom line, the dollar. They don't care about you, no matter what your color is. . . . If you're black or Latin or white, if they can set you up against the other workers, they're going to use you. They don't give a damn what color you are. It's the profit. 　　　JOE GUTIERREZ

The wealth of this country has to be divided differently. They play off one race against the other. That white kid on the picket line got the same problems as that black kid who don't have a job. . . . All the while, the corporate heads take the money and invest it in foreign countries. 　　JOSEPH ROBINSON

Racism is not an automatic thing. It's an organized prejudice against people. Racism, you just don't come out and be this way. It's got to be some motivation behind it, by telling people they're gonna lose the value of their house or this or that. I'm saying racism is unnatural. 　　FRANK LUMPKIN

Invisible racism

Racism is so universal in this country, so widespread and deep-seated, that it is invisible because it is so normal.
SHIRLEY CHISHOLM, 1970

As racism has become less visibly obvious since the 1960s, it has become easier for those not directly victimized by it to ignore it.
CLARENCE PAGE, 1996

The very absence of visible signs of discrimination creates an atmosphere of racial neutrality and encourages whites to believe that racism is a thing of the past.
DERRICK BELL, 1992

Today, racism is far more camouflaged than it was earlier in the century. It is buried in institutional practices. It is hidden in coded language and subtle messages some people get when they shop, or look for a place to live or for a taxi, or have dealings with the police.
PROJECT HIP-HOP, 1997

Students, research workers and professionals in the behavioral sciences — like members of the clergy and educators — are no more immune by virtue of their values and training to the diseases and superstitions of American racism than is the average man.
KENNETH B. CLARK, 1972

I'm beginning to feel that the greatest changes come from people who may hold an extreme position to begin with. . . . Where it's invisible is where the real trouble is. In the corporate board room, in the suburban setting, on the management level, where pretense is everything. It's not as visible as people throwing rocks, but may be potentially more damaging because it has a nice face on it.
JIM CAPRARO, 1992

The difference between de jure and de facto segregation is the difference between open, forthright bigotry and the shamefaced kind that works through unwritten agreements between real estate dealers, school officials, and local politicians.
SHIRLEY CHISHOLM, 1970

The code words differ. The message is the same.
DERRICK BELL, 1992

The very fact that no black leader could utter publicly that a black appointee for the Supreme Court was *unqualified* shows how captive they are to white racist stereotypes about black intellectual talent.

CORNEL WEST, 1993

Black people know that sometimes their greatest enemy is . . . white people of power who would never utter a racist sentence in public, yet who quietly and privately will do everything they can to keep black people as the slave class in this society.   CARL T. ROWAN, 1991

We [professionals] have moved on, but we cannot honestly say . . . that racism has moved into the past. It is harder to point to it now, people are more careful in what they say and maybe in what they think, too. And yet one senses it there, in the shadows, lurking perhaps around the next brightly lighted corner as one walks the corridor of one's office.   STEPHEN L. CARTER, 1993

Knowing that I would not be admitted to certain tournaments protected me from direct rebuffs. . . . No player ever refused to appear on court with me. No official ever called me a name. But the indirect rebuffs and innuendoes left their scars.   ARTHUR ASHE, 1981

If we tell ourselves that the only problem is hate, we avoid facing the reality that it is mostly nice, nonhating people who perpetuate racial inequality.

ELLIS COSE, 1997

Simply removing formal impediments to equality is not enough; the pecking order thrives on hidden power and invisible rules.

HARLON L. DALTON, 1995

The prejudices of centuries die hard, and even when they wane, the institutional frameworks that sustained them are bound to linger.

ORLANDO PATTERSON, 1997

Institutional racism is racism without a face.

CLYDE W. FORD, 1994

THE PAST

Negro men and women came here
long before the Mayflower
and they cleared the forests,
drained the swamps
and cultivated the grain.
The wealth of this country was founded
on what Abraham Lincoln called
"the 250 years of unrequited toil"
of Negro men and women.
From the muted wail of slaves
going in chains to American plantations
came the gold that made capitalism possible;
from black brawn came tobacco;
from black blood, white sugar.

LERONE BENNETT, JR., 1964

An invoice of ten negroes sent this day to John B Williamson by Geo Kremer named & cost as fol—lows

To wit .. Betsey Kackley . . . . $.410 . oo
    Nancy Aulick . . . . .515 . oo
    Harry & Helen Miller . . . 1200 . oo
    Mary Kootz . . . . 600 . oo
    Betsey Ott? . . . . 560 . oo
    Isaac & Fanny Brent . . 992 . oo
    Lucinda Luckett? . . . . . . 467 . 50
    George Smith . . . . 510 . oo

Amount of my traveling expences & boarding 5254 . 50
of lot No 9 not included in the other bills " 39 . 50
Kremers expences Transporting lot No 9 to Richmd 51 . 00
    Carryall hire . .   6 . 00
    $ 535? . 00

I have this day delivered the above named negroes costing including my expences and other expences five thousand three hundred & fifty dollars this May 26th 1835—

            John W Pittman

I did intend to leave Nancy child but she made such a damned fuss I had to let her take it I could of got fifty Dollars for so you must add forty Dollars to the above

Past history

The feeling of the nation
must be quickened;
the conscience of the nation
must be roused;
the propriety of the nation
must be startled;
the hypocrisy of the nation
must be exposed;
and its crimes against God and man
must be denounced.

FREDERICK DOUGLASS, 1852

CAUTION!!

COLORED PEOPLE
OF BOSTON, ONE & ALL,

You are hereby respectfully CAUTIONED and advised, to avoid conversing with the

Watchmen and Police Officers
of Boston,

For since the recent **ORDER OF THE MAYOR & ALDERMEN**, they are empowered to act as

KIDNAPPERS
AND
Slave Catchers,

And they have already been actually employed in **KIDNAPPING, CATCHING, AND KEEPING SLAVES.** Therefore, if you value your LIBERTY, and the *Welfare of the Fugitives* among you, *Shun* them in every possible manner, as so many *HOUNDS* on the track of the most unfortunate of your race.

Keep a Sharp Look Out for KIDNAPPERS, and have TOP EYE open.

APRIL 24, 1851.

Disinterring the past

The past isn't as remote as it seems, if you realize that there are people alive today whose grandparents were born as slaves. On the other hand, the recent past of segregation and the civil rights movement is ancient history to many young people.

Perhaps the very first thing we need to do as a nation and as individual members of society is to confront our past and see it for what it is. It is a past that is filled with some of the ugliest possible examples of racial brutality and degradation in human history. We need to recognize it for what it was and is and not explain it away, excuse it, or justify it.   JOHN HOPE FRANKLIN, 1993

The constant struggle between social and economic equality and the lust for profit . . . the battle of African-Americans for true freedom and a piece of the American dream . . . these themes have been with us for some time. And that they still trouble us is the best reason why knowing what those events were and what they mean is important in itself.
ALAN AXELROD / CHARLES PHILLIPS, 1992

We know White Supremacy is indefensible in today's world, we know that as an idea it is dead, but the bitter struggle goes on, South and North: wasting minds and time and hearts and economic resources, tying us to a past where ghost battles ghost.   LILLIAN SMITH, 1949

Some truths have to be really pounded into the national psyche. And one of them is that history counts.
ROGER WILKINS, 1998

The historical roots of American racism are conscious and deliberate, but sheer ignorance perpetuates it without any extra effort; most white Americans don't even know the history of slavery and the long continuing struggle of blacks to overcome it.

ANDREW YOUNG, 1996

There are complexities in every racial situation. Never are such matters neat and simple. They can't be. For they reach deep into history, memory, beliefs, values — or into the hollow place where values should be.

LILLIAN SMITH, 1949

We are what we are today because of what happened yesterday, and our todays will remain horrible for precisely as long as we avoid the necessary confrontation with yesterday.

LERONE BENNETT, JR., 1964

Confronting and knowing our collective history is important because it is what shapes present circumstances; we are racist today because we were racist yesterday. The forms and the dynamics of that racism will change over time, but the root is connected to the branch in a way that is present in the here and now.

CHARLES R. LAWRENCE III / MARI J. MATSUDA, 1997

The psychic and physical devastation that so marked slave and colonial systems echoes into our lives today . . . If we could but see a causal chain, a procession of events linked over time, it might teach us many lessons about the long-term consequences of violently exploiting humans as only capital.

PATRICIA WILLIAMS, 1997

The past was supposed to be safely buried; the most crude and blatant forms of prejudice had apparently been discredited many years ago. This assumption failed to reckon with the subtler formulations in which the same basic ideas now insinuate themselves.

ALEXANDER THOMAS, M.D., 1972

A society is always eager to cover misdeeds with a cloak of forgetfulness, but no society can fully repress an ugly past when the ravages persist into the present. America owes a debt of justice which it has only begun to pay.

MARTIN LUTHER KING, JR., 1967

Perhaps a brighter vision of our future can be inspired by a better understanding of our recent past.
ANDREW YOUNG, 1996

Slavery

From 1619 until 1863 — almost 250 years — the southern states of the U.S. practiced the legalized enslavement of black Africans and their descendants. This institution was supported by a claim on the three most powerful symbols of civilized society — God, science, and profit.

I will, in the name of humanity, which is outraged, in the name of liberty, which is fettered, in the name of the Constitution and the Bible, which are disregarded and trampled upon, dare to call in question and to denounce, with all the emphasis I can command, everything that serves to perpetuate slavery — the great sin and shame of America!

FREDERICK DOUGLASS, 1852

Certainly it was no accident that slavery was the major moral issue the signers of the Declaration [of Independence] failed to address when they proclaimed liberty, equality, and justice for all, and went home to oversee their slaves. Just as it is no accident that our public dialogue on race today is more a monologue of frustration and rage.

KAREEM ABDUL-JABBAR, 1996

[In a new production of *Uncle Tom's Cabin*] there is a slave auction done entirely in pantomime — far more harrowing than if it had been staged with some attempt at realism, because what we are witnessing is something unspeakable.

MARGO JEFFERSON, 1998

Slavery has always been the defining event of American society.
KAREEM ABDUL-JABBAR, 1996

The means . . . by which the African race now in this country have been reduced to Slavery, cannot affect us, since they are our property, as your land is yours, by inheritance or purchase and prescriptive right. You will say that man cannot hold *property in man*. The answer is, that he can and *actually does* hold property in his fellow all the world over, in a variety of forms, and *has always done so*.

You attempt to avert the otherwise irresistible conclusion, that Slavery was . . . ordained by God, by declaring that the word "slave" is not . . . to be found in the Bible. . . . It is well known that both the Hebrew and Greek words translated "servant" in the Scriptures, mean also, and most usually, "slave." The use of the one word, instead of the other, was a mere matter of taste with the translators of the Bible.

I endorse without reserve the much abused sentiment . . . that "Slavery is the cornerstone of our republican edifice;" while I repudiate, as ridiculously absurd, that much lauded but nowhere accredited dogma of Mr. Jefferson, that "all men are born equal." No society has ever yet existed . . . without a natural variety of classes. The most marked of these must, in a country like ours, be the rich and the poor, the educated and the ignorant.

Laws have been recently passed . . . making it penal to teach slaves to read. . . . If the slave is not allowed to read his bible, the sin rests upon the abolitionists; for they stand prepared to furnish him with a key to it, which would make it, not a book of hope, and love, and peace, but of despair, hatred and blood; which would convert the reader, not into a Christian, but a demon. To preserve him from such a horrid destiny, it is a sacred duty which we owe to our slaves, not less than to ourselves, to interpose the most decisive means.

The research and ingenuity of the abolitionists, aided by the invention of runaway slaves — in which faculty, so far as improvising falsehood goes, the African race is without a rival — have succeeded in shocking the world with a small number of pretended instances of our barbarity.

It is, and it always has been, an object of prime consideration with our slaveholders, to keep families together. Negroes are themselves both perverse and comparatively indifferent about this matter.

If pleasure is correctly defined to be the absence of pain . . . I believe our slaves are the happiest three millions of human beings on whom the sun shines. Into their Eden is coming Satan in the guise of an abolitionist.

JAMES HENRY HAMMOND, 1845

Selections from *The Ideology of Slavery* [FAUST]

A knowledge of reading, writing, and the elements of arithmetic, is convenient and important to the free laborer, who is the transactor of his own affairs, and the guardian of his own interests — but of what use would they be to the slave? These alone do not elevate the mind or character, if such elevation were desirable.

The slave is certainly liable to be sold. But, perhaps, it may be questioned, whether this is a greater evil than the liability of the laborer . . . to be dismissed by his employer, with the uncertainty of being able to obtain employment, or the means of subsistence elsewhere. With us, the employer cannot dismiss his laborer without providing him with another employer.

The line of a slave's duty is marked out with precision, and he has no choice but to follow it. He is saved the double difficulty, first of determining the proper course for himself, and then of summoning up the energy which will sustain him in pursuing it.

At least as much injury has been done and suffering inflicted by weak and injudicious indulgence, as by inordinate severity. He whose business is to labor, should be made to labor, and that with due diligence, and should be vigorously restrained from excess or vice. This is no less necessary to his happiness than to his usefulness. The master who neglects this, not only makes his slaves unprofitable to himself, but discontented and wretched. WILLIAM HARPER, 1852

It is the duty of society to protect all its members . . . The love of power, properly directed, becomes the noblest of virtues, because power alone can enable us to be safely benevolent to the weak, poor, or criminal. To protect the weak, we must first enslave them . . . Domestic slaves . . . require masters of some kind, whose will and discretion shall stand as a law to them, who shall be entitled to their labor, and bound to provide for them. This social organization begets harmony and good will instead of competition, rivalry, and war of the wits.

Economically, slavery is necessary to bring about association of labor and division of expenses. Labor becomes far more efficient when many are associated together, and the expenses of living are greatly diminished when many families are united under a common government. The socialists are all aiming to attain these ends by an unnatural association, let them adopt the natural one, slavery, and they would show themselves wise and useful men. GEORGE FITZHUGH, 1857

Most of us came here in chains and most of you came here to escape your chains. Your freedom was our slavery, and therein lies the bitter difference in the way we look at life.

JOHN OLIVER KILLENS, 1964

Slaveholders [are] a people whose men are proverbially brave, intellectual and hospitable, and whose women are unaffectedly chaste, devoted to domestic life, and happy in it . . . My decided opinion is, that our system of Slavery contributes largely to the development and culture of these high and noble qualities.

JAMES HENRY HAMMOND, 1845

[Thomas] Jefferson talked about slaves as "my family." Obviously if some family members owned other family members, it is not a family in a traditional sense. You keep having to answer the question, was Jefferson a good slave master? That's an oxymoron. There are no good slave masters.

JULIAN BOND, 1998

Sometimes there was brutality; sometimes there wasn't. But the whole system turned on violence.

EDWARD BALL, 1998

The "science" of slavery

Let us recall that the white man, in order to justify slavery and, later on, to justify segregation, elaborated a complex, all-pervasive myth which at one time classified the black man as a subhuman beast of burden.
ELDRIDGE CLEAVER, 1968

The negro . . . depends upon the white man to do his mental work . . . . He is by nature and habit a servant, not alone because of his long period of enslavement, but because of his mental inferiority.
HUBERT HOWE BANCROFT 1912

In order to justify slavery in a courageous new world which was spouting slogans of freedom and equality and brotherhood, the enslavers, through their propagandists, had to create the fiction that the enslaved people were subhuman and undeserving of human rights and sympathies. The first job was to convince the outside world of the inherent inferiority of the enslaved. The second job was to convince the American people. And the third job, which was the cruelest hoax of all, was to convince the slaves themselves that they deserved to be slaves.
JOHN OLIVER KILLENS, 1964

In its long and ugly history . . . white racism has improvised a thousand variations on two basic themes. The first is that black people are born with inferior brains and a limited capacity for mental growth. The second is that their personality tends to be abnormal, whether by nature or by nurture. . . . Both have served to sanctify a hierarchical social order in which "the Negro's place" is forever ordained by his genes and the accumulated disabilities of his past.
ALEXANDER THOMAS, M.D., 1972

An "educated" negro, like a "free negro," is a social monstrosity, even more unnatural and repulsive than the latter. . . . God has made the negro an inferior being, not in most cases, but in all cases, for there are no accidents or exceptions in His works. There never could be such a thing as a negro equaling the standard Caucasian in natural ability.
DR. JOHN H. VAN EVRIE, 1853

Racism has always been able to come up with a scientific veneer.
ANDREW HACKER, 1992

"Scientific·racism" . . . holds that various human groups exist at different stages of biological evolution. . . . Since the theorists who devised this scenario were white, it is not difficult to deduce the skin color of the front-runners and of those who will pursue them forever like figures on a Grecian urn.

ALEXANDER THOMAS, M.D.
1972

Too often of late the media have been flooded with studies purporting to "inform" us of the inherent . . . inferiority . . . of this or that group. . . . Those slavery manifestos are dusted right off and tidied up into neat statistical columns, with rows of impressive numbers dotted with decimal points, percentage signs hovering at the edges like so much filigree.

PATRICIA WILLIAMS, 1997

The brain of the Negro . . . is, according to positive measurements, smaller than the Caucasian by a full tenth; and this deficiency exists particularly in the anterior portion of the brain, which is known to be the seat of the higher faculties. History and observation, both teach that in accordance with this defective organization, the Mongol, the Malay, the Indian and Negro, are now and have been in all ages and all places, inferior to the Caucasian.

There is in the animal kingdom, a regular gradation in the form of the brain, from the Caucasian down to the lowest order of animals, and . . . the intellectual faculties and instincts are commensurate with the size and form. . . In animals where the senses and sensual faculties predominate, the nerves coming off the brain are large, and we find the nerves of the Negro larger than those of the Caucasian.

No black race . . . has been, or can be established at any great distance from the equator. Look at the bills of mortality . . . and you will see the proportion of deaths amongst the blacks, increasing as you go north, until you get to Boston . . . a cold climate so freezes their brains as to make them insane or idiotical.   JOSIAH C. NOTT, 1844

[In 1851] Samuel Cartwright published a paper in the *New Orleans Medical and Surgical Journal* which attempted to substantiate the association of blackness and madness by specifically identifying those psychopathologies to which Blacks alone were prey. He pinpoints two "illnesses" which he labels "Drapetomania, or the diseases causing slaves to run away" and "Dysaesthesia aethiopsis or hebetude of mind and obtuse sensibility of body — a disease peculiar to negroes — called by overseers, 'rascality'."
SANDER L. GILMAN, 1982

Whiteness was not based on natural, biological premises but on property and terror.
DAVID ROEDIGER, 1998

This tradition continued virtually undisturbed into the present century. In 1906, a professor of anatomy at Johns Hopkins concluded that "it is useless to elevate the Negro by education or otherwise, except in the direction of his natural endowments". . . . This myth is by no means dead.   ALEXANDER THOMAS, M.D., 1972

Rather than feel superior to the benighted psychiatrists of past generations, we should be reminded how easy it is to distort science in the service of racism.
ALEXANDER THOMAS, M.D.
1972

Professor Michael Levin of City College of New York . . . concisely outlined the evidence for racial differences in such traits as average intelligence, aggressiveness, and the willingness to sacrifice today for benefits tomorrow. . . . He concluded with a bold survey of the ways in which employment, education, and law enforcement policies should recognize the biology that underlies the divergent ways in which the races behave.

Professor Eugene Valberg . . . argued that unless black Africans are taught liberal nonsense by whites, they are completely at ease with the notion of racial differences in intelligence.
"RACE AND AMERICAN CIVILIZATION" CONFERENCE, 1994

Racial science . . . makes anyone who knows the great messy, unprovable contrary . . . unintelligent, uninformed, powerless, and naïve. . . . It narrows the debate to the property of (extra-intelligent) "experts" who wrap their opinions in the sheepskin of false "proof."
PATRICIA WILLIAMS, 1997

It's hard to keep one's concentration when, phoenix-like, the rooster of racial science rises every twenty years or so, in ever more seductive plumage, intent upon proving the lost link between the rising of the sun and its crowing loudly. Like clockwork, black people must put aside the activities of everyday life and subject ourselves to the cyclical inspection point of proving our worth, justifying our existence, and teaching our history, over and over and over again.   PATRICIA WILLIAMS, 1997

[The Negro's] physical organization, and the laws of his nature, are in perfect unison with slavery.
SAMUEL CARTWRIGHT, 1851

The aftermath of slavery

After the initial period of exultation that followed the Emancipation Proclamation in 1863, most blacks discovered that there was nowhere for them to go except back to the farms of their former masters to labor as sharecroppers.

Had white America really believed in its egalitarian declarations, it would have welcomed former slaves into its midst at the close of the Civil War. Indeed, had that happened, America would not be two racial nations today.

ANDREW HACKER, 1992

One of the most stupendous of the wrongs which the Negro has suffered was in turning the whole army of slaves loose in a hostile country, without money, without friends, without experience in home getting or even self-support. Their two hundred fifty years of unrequited labor counted for naught. They were free but penniless in the land which they had made rich.

But though they were robbed of the reward of their labor, though they have been denied their common rights, though they have been discriminated against in every walk of life . . . yet through it all they have been true: true to the country they *owe* (?) so little, true to the flag that denies them protection, true to the government that practically disowns them, true to their honor, fidelity and loyalty.

HENRY CLAY BRUCE, 1895

Even after emancipation, citizens who had been slaves still found themselves consigned to a subordinate status. Put most simply, the ideology that had provided the rationale for slavery by no means disappeared. Blacks continued to be seen as an inferior species, not only unsuited for equality but not even meriting a chance to show their worth.

ANDREW HACKER, 1992

To find the origins of the Negro problem we must turn to the white man's problem.

MARTIN LUTHER KING, JR., 1967

A hopeful period (that was to last only ten years) was heralded with the Reconstruction Acts of 1867 and followed by the 14th and 15th Amendments, which gave Negroes citizenship and the right to vote without regard to "race, color, or previous condition of servitude." During that period, Negroes attended school with whites and were elected to state legislatures as well as to Congress.

The "redeemers" . . . framed new laws aimed just as surely at disenfranchising blacks as the Reconstruction legislation had aimed at protecting them. Such pieces of legislation were called "Jim Crow" laws, taking their name from the antebellum minstrel show that had given the Confederacy its national anthem, "Dixie."

ALAN AXELROD /
CHARLES PHILLIPS, 1992

There has never been a period in America, before or since, when the climate of public opinion was favorable to the passage of national legislation of the breadth and scope of the Fourteenth and Fifteenth amendments. . . . The Reconstructionists . . . made . . . the first — and last — real attempt to bring the American Dream down from its parchment heaven to the hard and challenging earth of black hope.   LERONE BENNETT, JR., 1987

WALNUT STREET
THEATRE,

Box 50 cents —Pit 25 cents —Gallery 18 3-4 cents.
Doors will be opened at half after 6, and the Curtain
rise at a quarter after 7 o'clock, precisely.

On this occasion

Mr. J. R. SCOTT
AND
MR. HOWARD,
WILL APPEAR

Mr. RICE

As the Far Famed

Jim Crow

Will also appear, and discuss
10 New Subjects,
In his Fashionable Lyric Style.

Monday Evening,
JUNE 3, 1833.

Many black colleges were established in these years — but so were the Ku Klux Klan and uncounted secret white supremacist groups. In 1896, the Supreme Court hammered the nail in the coffin of Reconstruction with its decision in Plessy v. Ferguson establishing the principle of "separate but equal." This enabled the Jim Crow system of segregation, which lasted until the 1950s.

Black Americans throughout their history have always been challenged by the harsh and often brutal reality of institutional racism. As a system of unequal power, political racism led to the disfranchisement of African-Americans after the Reconstruction's brief experiment in democracy.   MANNING MARABLE, 1997

At the heart of the fractured soul of America is the frightening chasm of race.
MANNING MARABLE, 1997

Separate-but-equal marked the last stage of the white man's flight into cultural neurosis, and the beginning of the black man's frantic striving to assert his humanity and equalize his position with the white.

ELDRIDGE CLEAVER, 1968

What is so often forgotten in any discussion of the Negro's "place" in American society is the fact that it was only as a slave that he really had one. The post-slave society had no place for the black American, and if there were to be any area of the society where the Negro might have an integral function, that area would have to be one that he created for himself. The Jim Crow laws were the white South's attempts to limit the new citizen's presence and rights in the mainstream of society, and they were extremely effective.

LEROI JONES, 1963

It's well worth remembering that Jim Crow flourished during the very time that millions of Europeans entered the United States. A deeply racialized U.S. society transformed ignorant and impoverished immigrants . . . into white people. And as whites, European newcomers enjoyed access to the American transition belt of upward economic mobility.

NELL IRVIN PAINTER, 1998

We may decry the color-prejudice of the South, yet it remains a heavy fact. Such curious kinks of the human mind . . . cannot be laughed away, nor always successfully stormed at, nor easily abolished by act of legislature. . . . They must be recognized as . . . things that stand in the way of civilization and religion and common decency. They can be met in but one way — by the breadth and broadening of human reason.

W.E.B. DU BOIS, 1903

Sanctified by religion, justified by philosophy and legalized by the Supreme Court, separate-but-equal was enforced by day by agencies of the law, and by the KKK & Co. under cover of night.

ELDRIDGE CLEAVER, 1968

Our minorities alone are in a position to know what the fathers of our democracy were talking about.

SARAH PATTON BOYLE, 1962

W.E.B. Du Bois and Booker T. Washington espoused diametrically opposed philosophies regarding the advancement of Negroes after Reconstruction. Washington established Tuskegee Institute, for primarily vocational training. Du Bois advocated the entry into higher education of "the talented tenth" of the Negro population.

In all things that are purely social we can be as separate as the fingers, yet one as the hand in all things essential to mutual progress.
BOOKER T. WASHINGTON, 1895

No race has ever risen out of the shadows into the sunlight without fierce opposition. We have been no exception to the rule . . . but we shall win in the end, for we shall have God and justice and fair play on our side.
BOOKER T. WASHINGTON, 1899

No race can prosper till it learns that there is as much dignity in tilling a field as in writing a poem. It is at the bottom of life we must begin, and not at the top. Nor should we permit our grievances to overshadow our opportunities.

We shall constitute one-third and more of the ignorance and crime of the South, or one-third its intelligence and progress; we shall contribute one-third to the business and industrial prosperity of the South, or we shall prove a veritable body of death, stagnating, depressing, retarding every effort to advance the body politic.

It is important and right that all privileges of the law be ours, but it is vastly more important that we be prepared for the exercises of these privileges. The opportunity to earn a dollar in a factory just now is worth infinitely more than the opportunity to spend a dollar in an opera-house.   BOOKER T. WASHINGTON, 1895

Racism is still that hound of hell which dogs the tracks of our civilization.
MARTIN LUTHER KING, JR., 1967

The permanent scar

Every time a black man sits down to write a coming-of-age memoir he must drag after him hundreds of years of history. Race is still the subject.
JUDITH DUNFORD, 1998

Slavery continues to shape our lives more than a century after abolition because the link it forged between Blackness and inferiority, Blackness and subservience, Blackness and danger, has survived to this day.
HARLON L. DALTON, 1995

It would take the wisdom of the ages to see the profound impact that several centuries of preoccupation with undervaluing an entire race of people could have on the moral fiber of a nation, and on the national psyche.
JOHN HOPE FRANKLIN, 1993

Two hundred and forty-four years of slavery and nearly a century of institutionalized terrorism in the form of segregation, lynchings, and second-class citizenship in America . . . has left its toll in the psychic scars and personal wounds now inscribed in the souls of black folk.
CORNEL WEST, 1993

Blacks could care for the most prized possessions of white people — their children. They could prepare the item most crucial to whites' well-being — their food. Yet whites persisted in saying, and perhaps believing, that blacks were inherently irresponsible.
CARL T. ROWAN, 1974

Slavery and the postjuridical slavery that was Jim Crow are what make the Afro-American experience unique in America. The impact of these institutions was devastating, and it continues today — which, in the long duration of social history and the development of human institutions, is but a moment away from these tragedies.
ORLANDO PATTERSON, 1997

For years the Negro has been taught that he is nobody, that his color is a sign of his biological depravity, that his being has been stamped with an indelible imprint of inferiority . . . All too few people realize how slavery and racial segregation have scarred the soul and wounded the spirit of the black man.
MARTIN LUTHER KING, JR., 1967

What we might have become, we are not. What we are now is only half of what we might have been.
CHARLES H. KING, JR., 1983

That Americans of African origin once wore the chains of chattels remains alive in the memory of both races and continues to separate them.

ANDREW HACKER, 1992

I have met many families whose ancestors were enslaved by my family. I've apologized only to one of those families because I don't think that words are enough. . . . They're like a Band-Aid on the wound.

EDWARD BALL, 1998

It does not matter that contemporary Black folk were not personally enslaved so long as we carry the stigmata of those who were — dark skin. Similarly, it does not matter whether our White counterparts actually descended from slavemasters so long as they inherited from our culture the mind-set that made it possible for liberty-loving, God-fearing people to subordinate their fellow human beings.

HARLON L. DALTON, 1995

The fact, as chilling as it is unavoidable, is that many among the conservative elite seem tone-deaf on the issue of race. They can't see that our country's moral aspirations — to be "a city on a hill," a beacon of hope and freedom to all the world — seem impossible when one sees the despair of so many of those Americans who descend from slaves.

GLENN C. LOURY, 1997

In my eye, my frantic scramblings to become substantial, I imagine myself functionally insane, operating within the constraints of a society itself driven mad, made sick by its unresolved history of slavery and ongoing trauma of racism.

WANDA COLEMAN, 1993

Slavery's enduring legacy is that our "subhumanity" has been deeply imprinted in the American psyche.
HARLON L. DALTON, 1995

The enduring legacy

Slavery robbed our black
ancestors of trust and other
values of social glue as
much as it robbed them of
dignity.
CLARENCE PAGE, 1996

Many black people feel that
whites don't understand
just how great an atrocity
slavery was. . . . We lost
who we were as a people.
GERALD EARLY, 1997

We are where we are, with
the huge bloody problem
delicately referred to as
"race relations," because of
a history.
CHARLES R. LAWRENCE III /
MARI J. MATSUDA, 1997

Among the most pervasive aspects of the "race problem" is the perception many black citizens have that they are still excluded, whether physically or psychologically, from American society.

African-Americans had answered the country's every call from its infancy . . . . Yet, the fame and fortune that were their just due never came. For their blood spent, lives lost, and battles won, they received *nothing*. They went back to slavery, real or economic, consigned there by hate, prejudice, bigotry, and intolerance.
COLIN POWELL, 1995

From slavery to the present, the nation has never opened its doors sufficiently to give black Americans a chance to become full citizens. White Americans often respond that it rests with blacks to put aside enough of their own culture so they can be absorbed into the dominant stream. Blacks can only shake their heads and reply that they have been doing just that for several centuries, with very little to show for it.

It is white America that has made being black so disconsolate an estate. Legal slavery may be in the past, but segregation and subordination have been allowed to persist. Even today, America imposes a stigma on every black child at birth. ANDREW HACKER, 1992

The minorities have been confined to the city by a moat of bigotry.
SHIRLEY CHISHOLM, 1970

African-Americans see a clear distinction between their experience and that of the many immigrants, and their descendants, who take the "we made it, why couldn't they" attitude.

Born as others in the melting pot of America, we did not melt. Instead, we were strung out to mature in the slime of ghettoes; denied equal opportunities, our flesh and spirits wasted away into nothingness.

CHARLES H. KING, JR., 1983

Somebody asked us if we remembered seeing the Statue of Liberty as we pulled into the harbor. Tell you the truth, we didn't care too much about it. The Statue of Liberty was important to white European immigrants. It was a symbol to them. We knew it wasn't meant for us.

SADIE AND BESSIE DELANY, 1993

Other Americans, for the most part . . . are just Americans. But we are more than just Americans, not because of our color but because of how America exploited our color. We are different, not because we willed it, but because America set us apart from the rest of the community for special exploitation.

JOHN OLIVER KILLENS, 1964

Other immigrant groups came to America with language and economic handicaps, but not with the stigma of color. Above all, no other ethnic group has been a slave on American soil, and no other group has had its family structure deliberately torn apart.

MARTIN LUTHER KING, JR., 1967

The openings in the American society which were there for every successive immigrant group for more than a century were never there for Negroes.

HAROLD R. ISAACS, 1963

Like it or not, who we *were* has much to do with who we *are*.
TOM MORGANTHAU / MARK RAMBLER, 1997

It is impossible to ignore the devastating effect on "family values" of a system under which couples could be separated, and parents and children sold away from each other, at the will of the owner.

When I think of the many horrors of slavery, the destruction of the family strikes me as probably the worst. We are still facing the consequences of that destruction.
ARTHUR ASHE, 1993

The Negro family for three hundred years has been on the tracks of the racing locomotives of American history, dragged along mangled and crippled.
MARTIN LUTHER KING, JR., 1967

The terrible tragedy for most of us black Americans is that we have not recovered from those days of slavery when the "master" viewed family life as something too good, too civilized, or too costly to him, for black people to enjoy.
CARL T. ROWAN, 1974

The entire nation — but especially the Afro-American poor whose postslavery ancestors simply never recovered from the familial ethnocide — are paying the price of the rapacity and wickedness of Southern slaveholders, *and let no one forget it*.   ORLANDO PATTERSON, 1997

White people tend to berate blacks for the breakdown of black families, but they habitually deny their history of suppressing these bonds. . . . It *is* a major problem in the black community. But we all need to ask why this weed still grows. Its roots are slavery; it flourishes today on prejudice, injustice, and white supremacy. Deal with the roots and the weed dies, and maybe flowers will grow.   KAREEM ABDUL-JABBAR, 1996

Millions on millions of white Americans are unable to understand that slums, family disorganization and illiteracy are not the causes of the racial problem, but the end product of that problem.   LERONE BENNETT, JR., 1965

Segregationists love to quote hard, statistical percentages of illegitimacy among lower-class Negroes, but this is a blot on our escutcheon, not theirs. Among people of whom a large number still remember grandmothers raised in slavery, it is remarkable that so many endorse high standards of chastity, rather than that many still do not.   SARAH PATTON BOYLE, 1962

The Negro is deep in the psyche and soma of America.
LERONE BENNETT, JR., 1964

Recent history

We come from a people
. . . who didn't know which way north was,
didn't have a map to get there,
didn't know if they would have shoes
or food or comfort or housing
. . . or nurturing or support
but who said, "I believe I'm better than this,
and I will run on and see what the end's gonna be."
. . . who had nothing — nothing,
and out of nothing, made a bridge to today,
made a bridge so that your children
and your children's children
could walk across,
which is the same thing
that Dr. King did for us.

OPRAH WINFREY, 1998

The Southern way

The Southern white power structure apparently understood throughout the Jim Crow era that if this vicious system were to have any chance of surviving, we blacks would have to be made to some large extent willing co-keepers of our own prison.   RANDALL ROBINSON, 1998

Colonel Brookhart . . . warned me that I needed to be careful. Georgia was not New York. . . . I had to learn to compromise, to accept a world I had not made and that was beyond my changing. . . . The colonel was telling me, in effect, not to rock the boat, to be a "good Negro."
COLIN POWELL, 1995

For almost a century after the abolition of slavery, America's black population subsisted under a system of controls. In the South, physical force was blatant and unabashed. The whims of a sheriff, an employer, even the driver of a bus, could hold black lives in thrall.
ANDREW HACKER, 1992

"Mr. Rickey," [Clay Hopper] said, "do you really think a nigger's a human being?" Branch Rickey bristled momentarily. Then, as he tells it, "I saw that this Mississippi-born man was sincere . . . that this regarding the Negro as subhuman was part of his heritage, that here was a man who had practically nursed racial prejudice from his mother's breast, so I decided to ignore the comment."
CARL T. ROWAN, 1960

If our white folks apologized to us every time they should, they wouldn't have time to do anything else.
LANGSTON HUGHES, 1948

In the segregated South poor whites could be kept in check by rich whites simply by reminding them that they were not blacks, that even in their poverty they were higher in the pecking order than black Harvard professors or black millionaires.

ARTHUR ASHE, 1993

In most towns with one fountain, only the word *White* is painted on it. The town's white idiot can drink out of it but the town's black college professor must go thirsty on a hot August day.

LILLIAN SMITH, 1949

Democracy, like charity, really begins at home. With a mote in one's own eye, it is hard to remove the beam from another's. . . . The whole English-speaking Caucasian world . . . needs its eyes opened. They are full of the dust of race prejudice. Our own American Southland is almost blind as a result.   1945

The South is the land of what is isn't. It is the land of the great evasion. The land of the positive negative. The land of doing things backward. A Punch and Judy land, a tragi-comedy place where human beings block their own doorways.   1947

From all I can gather in the South, the average white person does not give a tinker's damn whether Negroes have available to them the same public treatment as is given an alien enemy. Any white Nazi prisoner during the war could drink out of a WHITE fountain. But not me. . . . And the shame of it is that nobody is ashamed.

1952

The shameless old, funny old, quaint, queer, bad-mannered, old South. I really think when Secretary [of State] Dulles gets through flying around the world teaching democracy to foreigners, he ought to make a little speaking trip through the South, and start teaching our white folks there how to be democratic, too.   1954

Slavery times are almost a hundred years gone, and freedom in theory is almost a century old. Why do so many Southern white people still behave in the same old-fashioned way, still talk and act as if social philosophies, Negro achievements, and world aspirations had not advanced beyond the 18th century?   1957

LANGSTON HUGHES

Terrorism relied for its effectiveness on the racism of genteel society.
ALAN WOLFE, 1998

From *Killers of the Dream* [LILLIAN SMITH, 1949]

Every little southern town is a fine stage-set for Southern Tradition to use as it teaches its children the twisting turning dance of segregation.

Bending, shoving, genuflecting, ignoring, stepping off, demanding, giving in, avoiding . . . . Children, moving through the labyrinth made by grownups' greed and guilt and fear. So we learned the dance that cripples the human spirit, we who were white and we who were colored . . . until the movements were reflexes and made for the rest of our life without thinking. Alas, for many white children, they were movements made for the rest of their life without feeling.

We clung to the belief . . . that our white skin made us "better" than all other people. And this belief comforted us, for we felt worthless and weak when confronted by Authorities who had cheapened nearly all that we held dear, except our skin color. There, in the Land of Epidermis, every one of us was a little king.

By the time I had learned that God is love I also knew that I was better than a Negro, that all black folks have their place and must be kept in it . . . that a terrifying disaster would befall the South if ever I treated a Negro as my social equal.

From the day I was born, I began to learn my lessons. . . . I learned to believe in freedom, to glow when the word *democracy* was used, and to practice slavery from morning to night. I learned it the way all of my southern people learn it: by closing door after door until one's mind and heart and conscience are blocked off from each other and from reality.

They who so gravely taught me to split my body from my mind and both from my "soul," taught me also to split my conscience from my acts and Christianity from southern tradition.

We fought hard against understanding, we tried to live in a fog, we could not bear to see what was becoming clearer each day: that race relations are part of the total human experience, not something history has set off in one corner of time.

I had learned that God so loved the world that He gave His only begotten Son so that we might have segregated churches . . . that white southerners are a hospitable, courteous, tactful people who treat those of their own group with consideration and who as carefully segregate from all the richness of life "for their own good and welfare" thirteen million people whose skin is colored a little differently than my own.

The Southerner clings to two entirely antithetical doctrines, two legends, two histories. . . . He is, on the one hand, the proud citizen of a free society and, on the other, is committed to a society which has not yet dared to free itself of the necessity of naked and brutal oppression. He is part of a country which boasts that it has never lost a war; but he is also the representative of a conquered nation.

An old black man in Atlanta . . . looked into my eyes and directed me into my first segregated bus. . . . His eyes seemed to say that what I was feeling he had been feeling, at much higher pressure, all his life. But my eyes would never see the hell his eyes had seen. And this hell was, simply, that he had never in his life owned anything, not his wife, not his house, not his child, which could not, at any instant, be taken from him by the power of white people. . . . And for the rest of the time that I was in the South I watched the eyes of old black men.

JAMES BALDWIN, 1961

I was an immature 15-year-old. . . . I grew up in a segregated society and I thought that was the way it was and that's the way it should be. . . [Now I want] to be the link between the past and the future. I don't want to pass this along to another generation.

HAZEL BRYAN MASSERY, 1997
Photographed taunting Elizabeth Eckford at Little Rock in 1957

The Negros' struggles and despairs have been like fertilizer in the fields of his humanity, while we, like protected children with all our basic needs supplied, have given our attention to superficialities.

SARAH PATTON BOYLE, 1962

Long ago I learned not to be proud I'm white, but I had never thought to be, as I am, ashamed.

SARAH PATTON BOYLE, 1962

Little Rock

When I watch news footage of the day we entered school guarded by the 101st soldiers, I am moved by the enormity of that experience. I believe that was a moment when the whole nation took one giant step forward.

We headed down a path from which there was no turning back, because when we thought of alternatives, the only option was living our lives behind the fences of segregation and passing on that legacy to our children.
MELBA PATILLO BEALS, 1994

What we know as the Civil Rights Movement was ignited by the Supreme Court's 1954 decision in Brown v. Board of Education of Topeka, which outlawed school segregation.

Three years later, after an egregious attempt, in the name of states' rights, to prevent the admission of nine black teenagers to Central High School in Little Rock, Arkansas, President Eisenhower ordered federal troops to escort the children to school through jeering and threatening crowds.

Throughout the ensuing school year, these incredibly courageous youngsters endured not only isolation and verbal taunts, but varying degrees of physical assault.

Forty years ago, a single image first seared the heart and stirred the conscience of our nation. . . . Elizabeth Eckford walked to this door for her first day of school, utterly alone. She was turned away by people who were afraid of change, instructed by ignorance, hating what they simply could not understand. And America saw her, haunted and taunted for the simple color of her skin, and in the image we caught a very disturbing glimpse of ourselves.   PRESIDENT BILL CLINTON, (September 25) 1997

Does anybody really think we wanted to go to Central High School because we wanted to sit next to white people? We wanted to go to Central High School because they were getting Rhodes Scholarships there. We wanted equal access to opportunities.

MELBA PATILLO BEALS, 1997

It was Little Rock that made racial equality a driving obsession in my life.
PRESIDENT BILL CLINTON, (September 25) 1997

The integration had stolen my sixteenth birthday. Later that night before I sobbed into my pillow, I wrote: *Please, God, let me learn how to stop being a warrior. Sometimes I just need to be a girl.*
MELBA PATILLO BEALS, 1994

All this pomp and circumstance and the presence of my eight colleagues does not numb the pain I feel at entering Central High School . . . . a place that was meant to nourish us and prepare us for adulthood. But, because we dared to challenge the Southern tradition of segregation, this school became, instead, a furnace that consumed our youth and forged us into reluctant warriors.
MELBA PATILLO BEALS, 1994

The most important part of the Little Rock story was . . . the magnificent courage and dignity these young people displayed. . . . Their *action* did more to win the sympathy and support of democratic-minded white people than all the speeches about "tolerance" that have ever been made. . . . As they walk through Jim Crow barriers to attend school . . . the world rocks beneath their tread.

Dear children of Little Rock — you and your parents and the Negro people of your community have lifted our hearts and renewed our resolve that full freedom shall now be ours. You are the pride and the glory of our people, and my heart sings warm and tender with love for you.
PAUL ROBESON, 1958

The man of the year for 1958 is a 16-year-old boy. He is Ernest Green, the first Negro to graduate from Central High School in Little Rock, Arkansas. . . . In his hands a high school diploma becomes a banner of singular glory . . . The dim wonder of "book learning" in the minds of countless slaves who dared not touch a book for fear of flogging lies in that diploma. . . And the dew of ancient pain moistened his diploma. . . Ernest Green's diploma is stamped with song and tied with a prayer.
LANGSTON HUGHES, 1958

The patter of their feet . . . is the thunder of the marching men of Joshua.
PAUL ROBESON, 1958

The civil rights movement

[Martin Luther King, Jr.]
and everything that he
represented, all the people
whose names never made
the history books, made it
possible for me to stand
and be who I am and take
over ownership of my life.
OPRAH WINFREY, 1998

Racism, war, and poverty
were anchors dragging on
our society, preventing us
from reaching our full
potential, as if anchors
from a nineteenth-century
sailing ship had been
attached to the space
shuttle. We accepted the
challenges of detaching
those anchors.
ANDREW YOUNG, 1996

In 1955, the Civil Rights Movement was waiting in the wings of history when Rosa Parks refused to give up her seat in a segregated bus. The ensuing bus boycott by the Negroes of Montgomery, Alabama, lasted more than a year and brought Martin Luther King, Jr., to the forefront of the struggle.

In the United States, on paper at least, the Constitution and Bill of Rights gave all Americans certain rights, including the vote and the right to be treated equally before the law. The Movement was about making those rights more than a piece of paper.   PROJECT HIP-HOP, 1997

We should not lose our sense of how the civil rights movement happened . . . In blurring, or ignoring, the context of the struggle, the veneration of Martin Luther King becomes devoid of depth and context, and the ability to use his model to renew the struggle for a just and equitable society is lost.   ANDREW YOUNG, 1996

Every single Negro who is worth his salt is going to resent any kind of slurs and discrimination because of his race . . . . Talk about "Communists stirring up Negroes to protest," only makes present misunderstanding worse than ever. Negroes were stirred up long before there was a Communist Party, and they'll stay stirred up long after the Party has disappeared — unless Jim Crow has disappeared by then as well.   JACKIE ROBINSON, 1949

Racism, war, and poverty were heavy burdens, to challenge injustice was an easy burden.
ANDREW YOUNG, 1996

The idea of "gradualism" in taking measures to alleviate the evils of segregation, the absence of voting rights, and other forms of discrimination began to fall on deaf ears.

There comes a time when the cup of endurance runs over, and men are no longer willing to be plunged into an abyss of injustice where they experience the blackness of corroding despair. I hope, sirs, you can understand our legitimate and unavoidable impatience.
MARTIN LUTHER KING, JR.
(Letter) 1963

There *is* no reason that black men should be expected to be more patient, more forbearing, more farseeing than whites; indeed, quite the contrary.
JAMES BALDWIN, 1963

There is nothing in the . . . legal guarantees of our full citizenship rights, which says that the Constitution is to be enforced "gradually" where Negroes are concerned. "Gradualism" is a mighty long road. It stretches back 100 long and weary years, and looking forward it has no end.
PAUL ROBESON, 1958

Nearly a century after the Emancipation Proclamation, Negroes are still in many ways enslaved by our system, and few of their leaders can hear the expression "move too fast" applied to their aching crawl toward full citizenship without yearning to chastise the offender.
SARAH PATTON BOYLE, 1962

I have almost reached the regrettable conclusion that the Negro's greatest stumbling block in the stride toward freedom is . . . the white moderate . . . who paternalistically feels that he can set the timetable for another man's freedom.

For years now I have heard the word "Wait!" It rings in the ear of every Negro with a piercing familiarity. This "Wait" has almost always meant "Never." It has been a tranquilizing thalidomide, relieving the emotional stress for a moment, only to give birth to an ill-formed infant of frustration.   MARTIN LUTHER KING, JR., (Letter) 1963

We were trying to transform America, not triumph over white folk.
ANDREW YOUNG, 1996

Martin Luther King, Jr., adopted Gandhi's principles of nonviolence. Participants in marches and demonstrations were trained to refrain from any physical response no matter how brutal the provocation.

Society needs nonviolent gadflies to bring its tensions into the open and force its citizens to confront the ugliness of their prejudices and the tragedy of their racism.

Lacking sufficient access to television, publications and broad forums, Negroes have had to write their most persuasive essays with the blunt pen of marching ranks. . . . More white people learned more about the shame of America, and finally faced some aspects of it, during the years of nonviolent protest than during the century before.　　　　　　　　MARTIN LUTHER KING, JR., 1967

I was living in Montgomery, Alabama, during the bus boycott . . . When I heard [Reverend King] was gonna get out of jail, me and some other white women wanted to see this smart-aleck nigger. I'm so thankful I went down there that day because I might have gone all my life just the way I was. When I saw all those people beating up on him and he didn't fight back, and didn't cuss like I would have done, and he didn't say anything, I was just turned upside down.　　　　　　　　PEGGY TERRY, 1992

When white freedom riders were brutalized along with blacks, a sigh of relief went up from the black masses, because the blacks knew that white blood is the coin of freedom in a land where for four hundred years black blood has been shed unremarked and with impunity.
ELDRIDGE CLEAVER, 1968

Out of the new unity and action vast monuments of dignity were shaped, courage was forged and hope took concrete form.

For the first time in his history the Negro . . . gained manhood in the nation that had always called him "boy."
MARTIN LUTHER KING, JR.
1967

The "I Have a Dream" speech is really a message of hope, whose effect was to comfort the disturbed, but not without disturbing the comfortable.
BERNICE A. KING, 1993

Only when fighting is a genuine alternative does the decision not to fight represent a higher ethic.
ANDREW YOUNG, 1996

Martin Luther King, Jr.: The peaceful warrior [1929-1968]

Above all, he brought a new and higher dimension of human dignity to black people's lives.   CORETTA SCOTT KING, 1983

The bullet that killed him . . . did incalculable damage to the United States of America.   BOB HERBERT, 1998

A thoughtful man and one of deep personal faith, his conscience called him into action for the soul of our Nation. He mobilized thousands of other brave and principled Americans — black and white, renowned and unknown — and began a crusade for justice that continues today. In sit-ins, marches, demonstrations, and boycotts, he and many others met violence with nonviolence and ignorance with determination. . . Pouring out his life in service, Dr. King made enormous and lasting contributions to improve the lives of millions of his fellow Americans.   PRESIDENT BILL CLINTON, 1998

By superimposing the image of the black preacher on the image of Gandhi, by adding songs and symbols with concrete significance in Black America, King transformed a spontaneous local protest [in Montgomery, Alabama] into a national passive resistance movement with a method and an ideology.
LERONE BENNETT, JR., 1987

Martin had the ability to make us feel as if we were more than our daily selves, more than we had been — a part of a beautiful and glorious vision that was enabling us to transcend ourselves. It was a marvelous quality he had, not ever fully captured on the printed page or in recordings, to lift the people to another place so that they could almost feel themselves moving. . . . The Nobel [Peace] Prize was more than a personal award . . . It was an acknowledgment of the struggles of all black Americans for survival and achievement during the long, arduous, and difficult century since emancipation.   ANDREW YOUNG, 1996

King's continuing significance to African-American people is that he and others . . . represented the very best within ourselves. Young African-American[s] . . . can take special pride in the memory of Martin, because through study and commitment to the continuing fight for equality, they will become "new Martins."   MANNING MARABLE, 1997

Martin Luther King, Jr.: From his three classics

Letter from the Birmingham Jail
August 1963

An individual who breaks a law that conscience tells him is unjust, and willingly accepts the penalty by staying in jail to arouse the conscience of the community over its unjustice, is in reality expressing the very highest respect for law.

I have heard numerous religious leaders of the South call upon their worshippers to comply with a desegregation decision because it is the *law*, but I have longed to hear white ministers say, "Follow this decree because integration is morally *right* and the Negro is your brother."

I Have a Dream
Speech, August 1963

The life of the Negro is still sadly crippled by the manacles of segregation and the chains of discrimination; one hundred years later, the Negro lives on a lonely island of poverty in the midst of a vast ocean of material prosperity.

When the architects of our republic wrote the magnificent words of the Constitution and the Declaration of Independence, they were signing a promissory note to which every American was to fall heir. . . . It is obvious today that America has defaulted on this promissory note insofar as her citizens of color are concerned. Instead of honoring this sacred obligation, America has given the Negro people a bad check . . . which has come back marked "insufficient funds."

I've Been to the Mountaintop
Speech, April 1968

The nation is sick. Trouble is in the land. Confusion all around. . . But I know, somehow, that only when it is dark enough, can you see the stars.

We are determined to gain our rightful place in God's world. . . We are saying that we are determined to be men. We are determined to be people. We are saying that we are God's children. And that we don't have to live like we are forced to live.

It's all right to talk about "long white robes over yonder," in all of its symbolism. But ultimately people want some suits and dresses and shoes to wear down here. It's all right to talk about "streets flowing with milk and honey," but God has commanded us to be concerned about the slums down here, and his children who can't eat three square meals a day.

The power and effectiveness of the Movement came from the combination of individual courage, strength in numbers, and the belief in the moral and political righteousness of the cause.

They are not fighting *people*, they are fighting a past that bars them from a life of freedom and responsibility. For them, only the uncreated future counts: they know they must help make it.   LILLIAN SMITH, 1961

If the inexpressible cruelties of slavery could not stop us, the opposition we now face will surely fail. We will win our freedom because the sacred heritage of our nation and the eternal will of God are embodied in our echoing demands.
MARTIN LUTHER KING, JR.
(Letter) 1963

There is nothing more majestic than the determined courage of individuals willing to suffer and sacrifice for their freedom and dignity.

MARTIN LUTHER KING, JR., 1958

Sparks from the flames of Birmingham leaped from ghetto to ghetto, igniting inflammable material that had been gathering for years, welding Negroes into a great black mass of livid indignation.

LERONE BENNETT, JR., 1964

The moment the blacks were let into the white world — let out of the voiceless and faceless cages of their ghettos, singing, walking, talking, dancing, writing, and orating *their* image of America and of Americans — the white world was suddenly challenged to match its practice to its preachments.   ELDRIDGE CLEAVER, 1968

I stood on the steps of the Lincoln Memorial [on August 28, 1963] looking toward the Washington Monument . . . There were three hundred thousand people there and everybody felt the same way. . . for that suspended, isolated few hours in time there was more love in that mall than the world has ever known. The galvanizing of what the civil rights movement was about occurred on that day.   SAMMY DAVIS, JR., 1989

The movement was the canvas upon which we painted the rest of our lives.
MARGARET BURNHAM, 1998

Just when the Movement had achieved most of its basic civil rights goals and was turning toward the problem of economic inequality, it was derailed by the Vietnam War. Only after much soul-searching did Martin Luther King, Jr., decide to follow his conscience and speak out against the war though it meant diverting attention from the Movement and its war on poverty. Dr. King was assassinated a year later.

The civil rights movement was a time when we thought: Maybe now it will finally happen. Maybe now our country will finally grow up, come to terms with this race mess. But it seems like the momentum was lost when the Vietnam War happened. It was like all the energy of the young people, and the focus of the country, got shifted away from civil rights.   BESSIE DELANY, 1993

A few years ago . . . it seemed as if there was real promise of hope for the poor — both black and white . . . Then came the build-up in Vietnam and I watched the program broken and eviscerated as if it were some idle political plaything of a society gone mad on war, and I knew that America would never invest the necessary funds or energies in rehabilitation of its poor so long as adventures like Vietnam continued to draw men and skills and money like some demonic destructive suction tube.

The bombs in Vietnam explode at home; they destroy the hopes and possibilities for a decent America. . . . I am disappointed with our failure to deal positively and forthrightly with the triple evils of racism, extreme materialism, and militarism. We are presently moving down a dead-end road that can only lead to national disaster.
                    MARTIN LUTHER KING, JR., (April) 1967

A nation that continues year after year to spend more money on military defense than on programs of social uplift is approaching spiritual death.
                    MARTIN LUTHER KING, JR.
                    (April) 1967

We dared to believe that America could be healed of the gangrene of racism.
ANDREW YOUNG, 1996

The modern civil rights revolution succeeded in establishing a mainstream taboo against overt prejudice and bigotry, but it was far less successful in creating an enduring consensus about the role of government in combating them.
CHRISTOPHER EDLEY, JR.
1996

I marched with Martin Luther King, but I was too young to really know what was going on, how bad it really was. . . . It's really amazing to realize what those people went through to enable us, within my lifetime, to have what we should have had anyway. Now it's all changing.
ANITA HERBERT, 1992

In light of how much of the Movement's "unfinished business" remains, we see the Movement as ongoing, as something in which we can take part.
PROJECT HIP-HOP, 1997

The splintering of the nonviolent Movement after Dr. King's murder was followed by an escalation of urban rioting, the rise to leadership of more militant activist leaders, and a white and conservative backlash that unraveled much of the progress that had been made.

After centuries of bloodshed and assaulted personhood, uncompensated toil and disdained talent, brave marches and protracted court cases, the American curtain in the 1960s was finally falling on de jure racial discrimination. But while this benchmark stride was seen as an important first step by many African-Americans, it was seen as an epoch-ending step by many whites.
RANDALL ROBINSON, 1998

By 1966, the walls of overt racial segregation in the South, encrusted with almost a century of regional law, had almost completely crumbled. . . . As the outer crust of American racism and oppression was falling away, deeper, more recalcitrant patterns of discrimination lay exposed before us: the very nerve and bone structure of American racism.
ANDREW YOUNG, 1996

The changes wrought by the struggles, court decisions, protests, and legislation of the decade did leave a lasting mark on American culture and society. . . . But . . . for the most part . . . civil rights leaders have felt that their energies in recent decades have been spent holding onto the gains of the past.
ALAN AXELROD / CHARLES PHILLIPS, 1992

We are afraid we might end up here with a mouthful of Civil Rights and an empty stomach.
WHITNEY M. YOUNG, JR., 1964

THE PRESENT

Lest you think you are no longer in danger
of coming across the sensibility
that made lawn jockeys . . . and other dregs
of so-called Black Americana fashionable,
look no further than Popongo:
a small stuffed gorilla
. . . dressed in the latest hip-hop fashions,
and his face . . . molded
so that it is only lacking the red lips
of the old "darkie" caricature.
. . . Give it either to a racist
you wish to express solidarity with
or an NAACP member
who you think is getting too complacent.

CONSTANTINE VON HOFFMAN, 1997

BEING BLACK
Racism and the individual

Being a Negro in America is not a comfortable existence.
It means being part of the company
of the bruised, the battered, the scarred, and the defeated.
Being a Negro in America
means trying to smile when you want to cry.
It means trying to hold on to physical life
amid psychological death.
It means the pain of watching your children grow up
with clouds of inferiority in their mental skies.
It means having your legs cut off,
and then being condemned for being a cripple.
It means seeing your mother and father
spiritually murdered
by the slings and arrows of daily exploitation,
and then being hated for being an orphan.
Being a Negro in America
. . . means being harried by day and haunted by night
by a nagging sense of nobodiness
and constantly fighting to be saved from the poison of bitterness.
It means the ache and anguish of living in so many situations
where hopes unborn have died.

MARTIN LUTHER KING, JR., 1967

The constant burden

Few members of a race that has oppressed another race can understand or appreciate the deep groans and passionate yearnings of those that have been oppressed.
MARTIN LUTHER KING, JR. (Letter) 1963

No white person, even when he wants to, can understand what it means to be a Negro living in the United States of America, any more than a non-combatant can understand what it means to be in action.
MARGARET HALSEY, 1946

The only way I could hope to understand anything about the plight of black people would be to wake up some morning in a black man's skin.
JOHN HOWARD GRIFFIN, 1977

What every black American knows, and whites should try to imagine, is how it feels to have an unfavorable — and unfair — identity imposed on you every waking day.
ANDREW HACKER, 1992

White people of good will can sympathize, but they can never really understand that hot feeling close to sickness that overwhelms a Negro with self-respect and with a real concern for the institutions of democracy when he or she arrives at a bus station to see signs on separate restrooms saying: FOR COLORED WOMEN and FOR WHITE LADIES.
RACHEL ROBINSON, 1960

What black people know to the marrow of their bones is that when whites discriminate against others on the basis of color, it does not matter in the slightest how much black people have worked, struggled, lifted themselves up by their bootstraps, or how many degrees they might hold.
JOHN HOWARD GRIFFIN, 1977

Being black in America is like being forced to wear ill-fitting shoes. Some people adjust to it. It's always uncomfortable on your foot, but you've got to wear it because it's the only shoe you've got. . . . Some people can bear the uncomfort more than others. . . . When you see some acting docile and some acting militant, they have one thing in common: the shoe is uncomfortable. It always has been and always will be.
JOSEPH LATTIMORE, 1992

There's a moving violation that many African-Americans know as DWB: Driving While Black.
HENRY LOUIS GATES, JR., 1995

I have come to know race as a sealed dwelling with windows but no doors. One can look out but never leave.
RANDALL ROBINSON, 1998

The sun rises and the sun sets on our blackness. . . . No man or woman escapes this blackness, for from the first cry of birth to the last sigh of death, black we are and black we shall be.
CHARLES H. KING, JR., 1983

Prior to 1954, we lived in an atmosphere of novocain. Negroes found it necessary, in order to maintain whatever sanity they could, to remain somewhat aloof and detached from "the problem."
ELDRIDGE CLEAVER, 1968

Being black is like skating on ice but not knowing the location of the thin places, going to war without weapons, holding a hand grenade and searching for a target beyond the ten-second interval allotted after pulling the pin.

To be black is a confusing proposition. Not the color itself, but the complexities brought to it by the cold, harsh realities of a nation filled with all-encompassing whiteness. We are caught in the briar patches of white power and institutional controls, and there is no escape.
CHARLES H. KING, JR., 1983

I couldn't believe I was going to spend the rest of my life fighting with people who hate me when they don't even know me. . . . Why should I have to keep getting my face smashed? Why did I have to prove what no white man had to prove?
SAMMY DAVIS, JR., 1989

Before that nameless prejudice . . . before that personal disrespect and mockery, the ridicule and systematic humiliation, the distortion of fact and wanton license of fancy, the cynical ignoring of the better and the boisterous welcoming of the worse . . . before this there rises a sickening despair that would disarm and discourage any nation save that black host to whom *discouragement* is an unwritten word.
W.E.B. DU BOIS, 1903

Death comes early to my people: the slow death of incurable depression, eyes closed to hope, blinded by the brilliance of well-to-do Caucasian twilights, the gleaming finery of white opportunism so long denied to those whose skins are tinted or tainted by color.
CHARLES H. KING, JR., 1983

Only a Negro understands the social leprosy that segregation inflicts upon him.
MARTIN LUTHER KING, JR., 1967

The American Negro . . . simply wishes to make it possible for a man to be both a Negro and an American, without being cursed and spit on by his fellows, without having the doors of opportunity closed roughly in his face.

W.E.B. DU BOIS, 1903

A pall of sadness hangs over my life and the lives of almost all African Americans because of what we as a people have experienced historically in America, and what we as individuals experience each and every day.

Segregation . . . left me a marked man, forever aware of a shadow of contempt that lays across my identity and my sense of self-esteem. . . . the shadow is always there; only death will free me, and blacks like me, from its pall.

ARTHUR ASHE, 1993

I doubt if the problems of our teeming ghettos will have a great chance to be solved until the white majority, through genuine empathy, comes to feel the ache and anguish of the Negroes' daily life.

There is very little in the life and experience of white America that can compare to the curse this society has put on color. . . . The central quality in the Negro's life is pain — pain so old and so deep that it shows in almost every moment of his existence.

MARTIN LUTHER KING, JR., 1967

Whites talked about the problems of blacks as though such burdens sprang from blackness, from the color of a person's skin. But for black people, the burdens come not from blackness but from white people's seeming inability to see beyond that color to the human individual within.

JOHN HOWARD GRIFFIN, 1977

What Negroes have wanted and needed was not to cease being Negroes, but to cease being "Negroes"; i.e., the possessors of an identity marked by their skin and their features which automatically and inescapably condemned them to total disability for life.

HAROLD R. ISAACS, 1963

I was for all practical purposes a made-in-America person. Yet the making itself had not convinced me that I was truly a part of the process that governed the society. Black and white, two colors, two origins, two destinies, that is what intervened in the midst of reflections on place for a young African in the south of Georgia.

MOLEFI KETE ASANTE, 1993

The feeling that you are in quicksand is inescapable in the quagmire of a racist society.
MOLEFI KETE ASANTE, 1993

I grew up aware that I was a Negro, colored, black, a coon, a pickaninny, a nigger, an ace, a spade, and other less flattering terms.
ARTHUR ASHE, 1981

Three was the age when I learned that I was black, the colored kid, monkey-child, different.
PATRICIA WILLIAMS, 1997

Every parent some time faces the problem of explaining the facts of life to his child. Just as inevitably, for the Negro parent, the moment comes when he must explain to his offspring the facts of segregation.
MARTIN LUTHER KING, JR. 1958

I know that no matter what I achieve, how hard I work, how much I contribute, how high my standards, how deep my values, how good my intentions — in the minds of too many who have the power to impact my life, the color of my skin relegates me to second class citizenship; that is and always will be a Constant Burden.
JEAN TUCKER MANN, 1997

We were walking down the tree-lined street [in Columbus, Nebraska] when suddenly we found ourselves in the midst of a sea of white faces pointing, snickering, whispering, and staring at us. . . . I was not a stranger to this mutual sense of otherness, but I was overwhelmed by the strength and lopsidedness of the feeling.
FAYE WATTLETON, 1996

As a child, every time I encountered prejudice — which was rubbed in your face, once segregation started under Jim Crow — I would feel it down to my core. I was not a crying child, except when it came to being treated badly because of my race. . . . In those instances, I would go home and sit on my bed and weep and weep . . . the tears streaming down my face.   BESSIE DELANY, 1993

When I was very young, before an impervious shell had been grown around me by both those who loved me and those who hated me, I thought grownups quite silly for making such fuss about a difference in human features that seemed no more important than any other. . . . A small child's logic soon to be crushed by an infectious malevolence that would make the color difference all-consuming and unique among human differences.
RANDALL ROBINSON, 1998

I am pleased that God made my skin black, but I wish He had made it thicker.
CURT FLOOD

Over and above the political, economic, sociological, and international implications of racial prejudices, their major significance is that they place unnessary burdens upon human beings.
KENNETH B. CLARK, 1963

You don't have to be as good as white people, you have to be *better or the best*. When Negroes are average, *they fail*, unless they are very, very lucky. Now, if you're average and *white*, honey, you can go far. Just look at Dan Quayle. If that boy was colored he'd be washing dishes somewhere.
BESSIE DELANY, 1993

Overnight the world looked different, it wasn't one color anymore. . . . It was as if I'd walked through a swinging door for eighteen years, a door . . . always secretly held open. But . . . when it finally hit me it was worse than if I'd learned about it gradually and knew how to move with it.
SAMMY DAVIS, JR., 1989

I get mad because they don't see *me*. They see black. I'm not trying to act like I'm better than anyone else, but they don't see that I'm fairly intelligent. That I have opinions on different things. All they see is that I'm black and all that goes with it.
TASHA KNIGHT, 1992

I was torn between two issues — colored, and women's rights. But it seemed to me that no matter how much I had to put up with as a woman, the bigger problem was being colored. People looked at me and the first thing they saw was *Negro*, not *woman*. So racial equality, as a cause, won my heart.
BESSIE DELANY, 1993

My God, what do we want? What does any human being want? Take away an accident of pigmentation of a thin layer of our outer skin and there is no difference between me and anyone else. All we want is for that trivial difference to make no difference.
SHIRLEY CHISHOLM, 1970

JUST imported from Africa, by Capt. RICHARDS and now on board his Sloop at Coentfes's-Dock, a parcel of very fine young healthy SLAVES, To be fold by HENRY C. BOGART, next Door to Mr. John Vanderfpiegle.----He has alfo Molaffes for Sale.

Our vices and degradation are ever arrayed against us, but our virtues are passed by unnoticed.
JOHN B. RUSSWURM, 1827

Psychological murder

Prejudice is more than an incident in many lives; it is often lockstitched into the very fabric of personality. In such cases it cannot be extracted by tweezers. To change it, the whole pattern of life would have to be altered.
GORDON ALLPORT, 1954

How much faith in education can be clung to by people whose minds have been raped. For three centuries, black people have been told by white people that they were intellectually inferior — and generations of blacks have believed it and acted accordingly.
CARL T. ROWAN, 1974

From birth to death, the Negro is handled, distorted and violated by the symbols and tentacles of white power, tentacles that worm their way into his neurons and invade the gray cells of his cortex. . . . The Negro not only dons a mask; he becomes, in many instances, the mask he dons.
LERONE BENNETT, JR., 1964

There was not, no matter where one turned, any acceptable image of oneself, no proof of one's existence. One had the choice, either of "acting just like a nigger" or of *not* acting just like a nigger — and only those who have tried it know how impossible it is to tell the difference.
JAMES BALDWIN, 1961

I learned not so much to turn the other cheek as to present, wherever possible, no cheek at all. . . . I learned in moments of humiliation to walk away with what was left of my dignity, rather than lose it all in an explosion of rage.
ARTHUR ASHE, 1993

Black folks aren't born expecting segregation, prepared from day one to follow its confining rules. Nobody presents you with a handbook when you're teething and says, "Here's how you must behave as a second-class citizen." Instead, the humiliating expectations and traditions of segregation creep over you, slowly stealing a teaspoonful of your self-esteem each day.
MELBA PATILLO BEALS, 1994

Where does a black soul go to rest?
RANDALL ROBINSON, 1998

Because the society, with unmitigated cruelty, has made the Negro's color anathema, every Negro child suffers a traumatic emotional burden when he encounters the reality of his black skin.
MARTIN LUTHER KING, JR. 1967

Conscious submission to racism seemed to me worse than death. It killed a person's spirit. It took a little from him each time he knew he should not submit — and did.
JAMES FORMAN, 1972

Racism ultimately created the state in which defensiveness and hypocrisy are our almost instinctive responses, and innocence and generosity are invitations to trouble.
ARTHUR ASHE, 1993

The blacks bore lifetimes of insults quietly like ancient scars, most of them insults casually, rather than wilfully, inflicted, tossed at them by whites operating under the foolish assumptions of racism. Even to be talked to fondly, like a favorite hound, can leave a mark, and the black people bore up under this marking until they were psychologically a tattooed people.
MELISSA FAYE GREENE, 1991

Struggle is the essence of life for us, yet the form of struggle makes a difference in the psychology of the individual. I have often wished that our struggle could somehow be less agonized, less emotionally complex . . . with more promise of clear victory than we have seen after four hundred years of sacrifice and death.
JAMES FORMAN, 1972

I knew . . . that in trying to shut the Negro race away from us, we have shut ourselves away from so many good, creative, honest, deeply human things in life . . . that the warped, distorted frame we have put around every Negro child from birth is around every white child also . . . that what cruelly shapes and cripples the personality of one is as cruelly shaping and crippling the personality of the other.
LILLIAN SMITH, 1949

A social system in which "white is right" presents a serious threat to the self-esteem of black Americans. . . There is thus abundant psychological justification for the new emphasis on black pride. Teaching children that "black is beautiful" is a healthy corrective to the lesson long inculcated by white society that black is blemished.
ALEXANDER THOMAS, M.D., 1972

My emerging personality has been pressed hard against the color-conscious society's rigid contour.
RANDALL ROBINSON, 1998

Racial identity

Your real work as a Negro lies in two directions: *First*, to let the world know what there is fine and genuine about the Negro race. And *secondly*, to see that there is nothing about that race which is worth contempt; your contempt, my contempt; or the contempt of the wide, wide world.

W.E.B. DU BOIS, 1928

"I really don't think of you as Black." . . . The erasure of my Blackness is meant to be a compliment, but I am not flattered. For when I am e-raced, I am denied an identity that is meaningful to me and am separated from people who are my flesh and blood.

HARLON L. DALTON, 1995

Black awareness is the essential beginning step in creating a framework for understanding and accomplishing the educational and political work that values our humanity. Real empowerment begins by learning the lessons of our own heritage and knowing something about ourselves.

MANNING MARABLE, 1997

The cornerstone of identity in the African American world was the knowledge that we as a people had been historically wronged by the larger culture that dominated us. We believed that we were morally superior to that culture because it was only a misfortune to be a slave but a shame and a sin to be the owner of slaves.

ARTHUR ASHE, 1993

Black Americans are tied to each other in ways that the majority cannot begin to presume to understand.

ANTHONY WALTON, 1993

The Afro-American identity movements and some form of affirmative action were the inevitable social fires that had to be ignited in the fight against the centuries-long holocaust of Euro-American racism.

ORLANDO PATTERSON, 1997

The quest for black identity involves self-respect and self-regard, realms inseparable from, yet not identical to, political power and economic status.

CORNEL WEST, 1993

If men despise Negroes, they will not despise them less if [they] are called "colored" or "Afro-Americans."

W.E.B. DU BOIS, 1928

If society says it is better to be white, not only white people but Negroes come to believe it. And a child may try to escape the trap of inferiority by denying the fact of his own race.

KENNETH B. CLARK, 1963

Not many Negroes were impressed by the [Black] Muslims' call for total separation. But almost all Negroes were touched by their savage indictment of hypocrisy and their delicious acceptance of the fact of being black.

LERONE BENNETT, JR., 1964

Like it or not, a black man, unless he has become irretrievably "white-minded," responds with an additional dimension of his being to the articulated experience of another black — in spite of the universality of human experience.

ELDRIDGE CLEAVER, 1968

Identity is so much a part of human nature that its significance is too easily minimized. Nowhere is this tendency to take identity for granted more dramatic than in the touchy area of race.

The cloak of proud black identity has provided a therapeutic warmth for my naked self after the chilly cocoon of inferiority imposed early in my life by a white-exalting society. But it is best worn loosely, lest it become as constricting and isolating for the famished individual soul as the garment it replaced.

Black folks still tell me how to be "black" when I stray from the racial party lines, while white folks tell me how to be "color-blind." I still feel as frustrated in my attempts to transcend race as a reluctant lemming must feel while being rushed over the brink by its herd.

CLARENCE PAGE, 1996

Completely by the accident of racism, we have been bound together with people with whom we may or not have something in common, just because we are "black." One day you wonder: What do the misdeeds of a Mike Tyson have to do with me? So why do I feel implicated? And how can I not feel racial recrimination when I can feel racial pride?

HENRY LOUIS GATES, JR., 1994

I am made "black" only in the most superficial way by virtue of being the object of a white racist's hate. The empathetic exchange of survivors' tales among "brothers," even the collective struggle against the clear wrong of racism, does not provide a tapestry sufficiently rich to give meaning and definition to the totality of my life.

GLENN C. LOURY, 1993

I learned it was possible, even desirable, to have a black identity without being poor.
ANDREW YOUNG, 1996

Weak as its scientific foundation may be, race is an essential part of who we are (and of how we see others) that is no more easily shed than unpleasant memories. Few of us would choose to be rendered raceless — to be suddenly without a tribe.   ELLIS COSE, 1997

Though it is no longer fashionable to say it, I am obsessively black. Race is an overarching aspect of my identity. America has made me this way. Or, more accurately, white Americans have made me this way.
                    RANDALL ROBINSON, 1998

While [blacks] were ashamed of their color, it was an albatross hanging around their necks. They freed themselves from that dead weight by picking up their blackness and holding it out proudly for all the world to see. They found their own beauty and turned their former shame into their badge of honor.   SHIRLEY CHISHOLM, 1970

One's racial identity can be a source of either pride or shame, according to the individual. I choose the former over the latter.
                    KEILI LANGFORD, 1998

Do I need to appear "Black," in the manner in which blacks are negatively portrayed in the media, to be considered "Black"? . . . I am an educated, well-spoken black woman. My race is one of my many attributes: neither limiting, nor defining. I represent the culmination of my experiences, and the many cultures that have influenced me. I represent the colors of my ancestors. But most of all, I represent myself, and of that, I am most proud.
                    RENEE DELPHIN, 1997

Color is not a human or a personal reality; it is a political reality.
                    JAMES BALDWIN, 1963

Living in two worlds

One ever feels his two-ness — an American, a Negro; two souls, two thoughts, two unreconciled strivings; two warring ideals in one dark body, whose dogged strength alone keeps it from being torn asunder.
W.E.B. DU BOIS, 1903

To be a Negro in America . . . means fighting daily a double battle — a battle against pathology within and a battle against oppression without.
MARTIN LUTHER KING, JR. 1967

It is a fact — though few of the dominant race have the imagination to realize it — that the life of a Negro . . . must always be lived in the United States on two planes. This double existence too often creates below the surface a deadly war of shame and blame.
ELIZABETH SHEPLEY SERGEANT, 1927

Like so many other people who have become members of the American society, Negroes have to blend their unique character as a group with the common character they share as Americans. Between these two identifications there has been up to now a deep and mutually deforming split.
HAROLD R. ISAACS, 1963

There were times . . . when I felt a burning sense of shame that I was not with other blacks — and whites — standing up to the fire hoses and the police dogs . . . As my fame increased, so did my anguish. I knew that many blacks were proud of my accomplishments on the tennis court. But I also knew that some others . . . did not bother to hide . . . their disdain and contempt for me.
ARTHUR ASHE, 1993

As a black professional in America it is sometimes so difficult to find true acceptance in either the black or the white communities that I often feel like an outsider to both; alienation seems to be the price of living with a foot in each world.
LAWRENCE OTIS GRAHAM, 1995

I sit with Shakespeare and he winces not. Across the color-line I move arm in arm with Balzac.
W.E.B. DU BOIS, 1903

The very act of constantly dividing one's personality between a predominantly white world of work and a predominantly black home community can be wearying.

CLARENCE PAGE, 1996

Paranoia becomes a way of life as black personalities become dichotomous. Living in a white world is like skating on thin ice. A hypocritical posture of well-being and adjustment must be projected lest the full dimension of inner black thoughts and feelings disrupt white illusions and perspectives.

What I found on those [dominantly white] campuses is . . . black faces popping up in an ocean of white milk. Black students, submerged in both numbers and potential, living two lives. The retreat from white customs and traditions into the solidarity of blackness was occasioned by establishing a black house on campus. This separate world within the white world was the only means of escaping the trauma induced by racism.

CHARLES H. KING, JR., 1983

The ability to remain true to *one* self . . . must begin with the ethical project of considering how we can align a sense of ourselves with a sense of the world. This is the essence of integrity, is it not, never having to split into a well-maintained "front" and a closely guarded "inside."

In its most literal sense, the ability to be one person rather than two refers to some resolution of the ethically dangerous position of finding oneself split between the one one is and the one one feels one *has* to be. The sheltered self and the masquerade.

PATRICIA WILLIAMS, 1997

No matter how liberal, how well accepted into the white community, no matter how popular or famous, no matter how unprejudiced a Negro may be, most of us have to wear some sort of mask outside our own group.

ALTHEA GIBSON

The fact that blacks were dichotomous out of the need for psychic and emotional survival was a truth that, either known or unknown, was denied by whites.

CHARLES H. KING, JR., 1983

There's that clunky social *box*, larger than your body, taking up all that space. You need two chairs at the table, one for you, one for your blackness.

PATRICIA WILLIAMS, 1997

Blacks and whites see the world differently because they live in different worlds.

CHRISTOPHER EDLEY, JR., 1996

Fear and rage

With the passage of time, I became increasingly aware of how all the adults around me . . . were living with constant fear and apprehension. It felt as though we always had a white foot pressed against the back of our necks.
MELBA PATILLO BEALS, 1994

All our efforts to make ourselves acceptable Negroes could not keep us safe. In a confrontation with white authority, the odds were clearly against us.　ANDREW YOUNG, 1996

My son was turning three years old. . . . Somewhere along the way he is going to turn almost overnight from someone who is perceived as cute and innocent into someone who is perceived as a menace, the most feared creature on America's urban streets today, *a young black male.*
CLARENCE PAGE, 1996

The constant danger which enshadows the Negro American all his life — danger of small and great indignities, and of actual physical harm or outright destruction — is something that cannot be conveyed to those who have not lived through it.　MARGARET HALSEY, 1946

The fear that I heard in my father's voice . . . when he realized that I really *believed* I could do anything a white boy could do, and had every intention of proving it, was not at all like the fear I heard when one of us was ill. . . . It was another fear, a fear that the child, in challenging the white world's assumptions, was putting himself in the path of destruction.　JAMES BALDWIN, 1963

I was eight years old when I saw a photo of Emmett Till's body. . . . The murder shocked me; I began thinking of myself as a black person for the first time, not just a person. And I grew more distrustful and wary. . . . I could be hurt or even killed just for being black.
KAREEM ABDUL-JABBAR, 1996

How frustrating it is for those who think they have reached the dream of equal opportunity, dignity, and acceptance, only to discover it fading into a nightmare of guilt, fear, suspicion, and resentment. Whether we actually are *subjected* to contempt or not, we are enraged by the very vulnerability that makes us forever *subject* to it.
CLARENCE PAGE, 1996

The choice is between ventilated rage and silence. We choose silence.
RANDALL ROBINSON, 1998

The accumulated effect of the black wounds and scars suffered in a white-dominated society is a deep-seated anger, a boiling sense of rage, and a passionate pessimism regarding America's will to justice.   CORNEL WEST, 1993

It's hard enough to be a human being under any circumstances, but when there is an entire civilization determined to stop you from being one, things get a little more desperately complicated. What do you do then?   LEROI JONES, 1961

The fire in my bones achieves white heat, consuming my joy at individual successes, stunting the growth of love toward all who are not of my hue, stifling the very air considered to be free.
CHARLES H. KING, JR., 1983

If people can understand what motivates Jackie Robinson, what makes him appear in moments of crisis to be consumed by rage . . . [they] may also find a better understanding of the forces with which [Negroes] grapple throughout the world today.   CARL T. ROWAN, 1960

In a democracy . . . a segregated minority is going to hate its segregators just as sure as God made little apples. This is not Negro nature, but human nature, which resents false promises a good deal more intensively than it resents no promises at all.   MARGARET HALSEY, 1946

You cannot deny people the basic emotions of rage, resentment and, yes, hate. Only slaves or saints or masochists love their oppressors. If you humiliate a man, if you degrade him, if you do this over and over for hundreds of years, he will either hate you or hate himself. This is a basic fact of humanity, and Negroes are human.
LERONE BENNETT, JR., 1964

God help me if I ever decide that there is no course left but that of destruction. I can feel in myself sometimes an anger that wants only to destroy everything in its path. There is a point at which passions as great as those that burn in the hearts of black Americans will not be frustrated any longer.   SHIRLEY CHISHOLM, 1970

It cannot be taken for granted that Negroes will adhere to nonviolence under any and all conditions. When there is rocklike intransigence or sophisticated manipulation that mocks the empty-handed petitioner, rage replaces reason.   MARTIN LUTHER KING, JR., 1967

It would be years before I understood the emotional toll of repressing anger and natural frustration.
ARTHUR ASHE, 1981

There is a fire in my bones. It is there because of the problem of race. I speak of race as a condition, not as a state of being. The black of me has now become the whole of me. It has not always been thus. The flames of hate and hostility toward white America developed slowly — burning all vestiges of accommodation or subjugation to whiteness. I am now a man.

White institutions make of me a warrior, ready to do battle, hammering incessantly against those practices and customs that eat the heart out of my existence. What you have not known, cruel white world, is the steel beneath my sinew and muscles, and the untapped reservoir of my brain.   CHARLES H. KING, JR., 1983

The Los Angeles cops acted out their racist nature on one more black man. They beat, tortured, persecuted me until my nerves snapped and those bright white lights seared my mind asunder. . . . If I had my way, I have thought many times in the years since then, I would line these criminals against the wall and coolly, coldly, with calculated aim, shoot all of them through the icy blue of their murderous eyes.   JAMES FORMAN, 1972

Malcolm X articulated black rage in a manner unprecedented in American history. . . . The substance of what he said highlighted the chronic refusal of most Americans to acknowledge the sheer absurdity that confronts human beings of African descent in this country — the incessant assaults on black intelligence, beauty, character, and possibility.   CORNEL WEST, 1993

I think that rage is an understandable and appropriate response to an absurd situation, namely, black people finding themselves in a situation of white supremacist power.
CORNEL WEST, 1997

The anger of the oppressed man is a sign of health, not pathology. It says: "I am condemning you for doing wrong to me."
ALEXANDER THOMAS, M.D.
1972

The most dangerous creation of any society is that man who has nothing to lose.
JAMES BALDWIN, 1963

Malcolm X: The embodiment of black rage

Debate, with James Farmer
March 1962

We who are Muslims . . . don't think that an integrated cup of coffee is sufficient payment for 310 years of slave labor.

Second-class citizenship is only a modified form of slavery, which means the Civil War didn't end slavery and the Amendments didn't end slavery. They didn't do it because we still have to wrestle the Supreme Court and the Congress and the Senate to correct the hypocrisy that's been practiced against us by whites for the past umteen years.

The Autobiography of Malcolm X, 1964-5

Human rights! Respect as *human beings*! That's what America's black masses want. That's the true problem. The black masses want not to be shrunk from as though they are plague-ridden. They want not to be walled up in slums, in the ghettoes, like animals. They want to live in an open, free society where they can walk with their heads up, like men, and women!

Is white America really sorry for her crimes against the black people? Does white America have the capacity to repent — and to atone? Does the capacity to repent, to atone, exist in a majority, in one-half, in even one-third of American white society?. . . Indeed, how *can* white society atone for enslaving, for raping, for unmanning, for otherwise brutalizing *millions* of human beings, for centuries? What atonement would the God of Justice demand for the robbery of the black people's labor, their lives, their true identities, their culture, their history — and even their human dignity?

Where the really sincere white people have got to do their "proving" of themselves is not among the black *victims*, but out in the battle lines of where America's racism really *is* — and that's in their own communities.

Sometimes, I have dared to dream . . . that one day, history may even say that my voice — which disturbed the white man's smugness, and his arrogance, and his complacency . . . helped to save America from a grave, possibly even a fatal catastrophe.

The goal has always been the same, with the approaches to it as different as mine and Dr. Martin Luther King's . . . that dramatizes the brutality and the evil of the white man against defenseless blacks. And in the racial climate of this country today, it is anybody's guess which of the "extremes" in approach to the black man's problems might *personally* meet a fatal catastrophe first — "non-violent" Dr. King, or so-called "violent" me.

Malcolm X: Controversial rebel [1925-1965]

I . . . refuse to be put in the position of denying the truth of Malcolm's statements simply because I disagree with his conclusions.   JAMES BALDWIN, 1963

Malcolm . . . was refreshing excitement; he scared hell out of the rest of us, bred as we are to caution, to hypocrisy in the presence of white folks, to the smile that never fades. . . Whatever else he was — or was not — *Malcolm was a man*!   OSSIE DAVIS, 1965

Malcolm X sharply crystallized the relation of black affirmation of self, black desire for freedom, black rage against American society, and the likelihood of early black death. . . . the first real black spokesperson who looked ferocious white racism in the eye, didn't blink, and lived long enough to tell America the truth.   CORNEL WEST, 1993

Although Malcolm X was assassinated before he could organize his ideas into a movement, he was an enormously talented theorist who influenced millions with his articulate expositions on television programs and his lectures on public platforms.
    LERONE BENNETT, JR., 1987

Because of his untimely death, Malcolm X bequeathed to the cause of civil rights an incomplete legacy open to wide interpretation. Many whites saw his transformation from hatred and anger to a religiously inspired quest after racial equality as a hopeful sign. . . .

Militant blacks emphasized Malcolm X's earlier message that only blacks could free themselves.
    ALAN AXELROD / CHARLES PHILLIPS, 1992

Malcolm X, in the eyes of Elijah's [Muslim] followers, had committed the unforgivable heresy when, changing his view and abandoning the racist position, he admitted the possibility of brotherhood between blacks and whites.   ELDRIDGE CLEAVER, 1968

Even had Malcolm not changed, he would still have been a relevant figure on the American scene, standing in relation . . . to the "responsible" civil rights leaders, just about where John Brown stood in relation to the "responsible" abolitionists . . . One final salute to that brave, black, ironic gallantry, which was his style and hallmark, that shocking *zing* of fire-and-be-damned-to-you, so absolutely absent in every other Negro man I know.
    OSSIE DAVIS, 1965

Beyond rage and hate

The sins of the fathers are visited upon the heads of the children — but only if the children continue in the evil deeds of the fathers.
ELDRIDGE CLEAVER, 1968

Hate is just as injurious to the hater as it is to the hated. Like an unchecked cancer, hate corrodes the personality and eats away its vital unity. . . . Hate is too great a burden to bear.
MARTIN LUTHER KING, JR. 1967

It demands great spiritual resilience not to hate the hater whose foot is on your neck, and an even greater miracle of perception and charity not to teach your child to hate.
JAMES BALDWIN, 1963

I want to say to every African-American living in this country and abroad, who holds, like, one teeny little piece of bitterness in your heart, you need to let it go and live on the legacy.
OPRAH WINFREY, 1998

I esteem myself a good, persistent hater of injustice and oppression, but my resentment ceases when they cease, and I have no heart to visit upon children the sins of their fathers.
FREDERICK DOUGLASS, 1881

My father . . . told us that the men who burned down our farm were not three white men. They were individuals with hatred and jealousy in their hearts. He implored us not to label or stereotype anyone based on the color of their skin. My father further warned us not to become embittered by other people's hatred because it would poison our lives as it had the lives of those three men.
ARMSTRONG WILLIAMS, 1997

I . . . must oppose any attempt that Negroes may make to do to others what has been done to them. I think I know . . . the spiritual wasteland to which that road leads. It is so simple a fact and one that is so hard, apparently, to grasp: *Whoever debases others is debasing himself.*
JAMES BALDWIN, 1963

Nothing can ever justify the articulation of hatred. Color prejudice transcends the barriers of black and white. The great strength of the black freedom movement . . . has been the realization that our struggle for equality is not just for ourselves, but for all humanity. When we surrender this moral and ethical principle, we sacrifice our greatest weapon in the battle for democracy for all people who experience discrimination.
MANNING MARABLE, 1997

The price of hating other human beings is loving oneself less.
ELDRIDGE CLEAVER, 1968

Overcoming

We come from a legacy of people who, when they were told they were nothing and everything around them, every single experience in their life, said, "You are nobody. You are nothing". . . . somewhere inside themselves, said, "I believe I'm better."

OPRAH WINFREY, 1998

The reason I don't feel anger is because the white man's not keeping his foot on my mind. He can't do anything to my mind. I'm free to think whatever I want to think. He's afraid, but he doesn't know he's afraid.

CAROL FREEMAN, 1992

By age thirteen, I had intuitively developed the cardinal guidepost for emotional health: the Never Wannabe Rule. Never want to be with people who don't want to be with you.

RANDALL ROBINSON, 1998

The Negro will only be truly free when he reaches down to the inner depths of his own being and signs with the pen and ink of assertive selfhood his own emancipation proclamation. . . . The Negro must boldly throw off the manacles of self-abnegation and say to himself and the world: "I am somebody. I am a person. I am a man with dignity and honor."   MARTIN LUTHER KING, JR., 1967

We were neither trained nor expected to protest against racial injustice, for that was not considered possible, or even desirable. . . . It was wisdom that would enable us to survive, not courage or the unpleasant and uncomfortable emotions evoked by honesty.

ANDREW YOUNG, 1996

Under conditions of slavery, enforced backwardness, oppression, and debasement, Negroes in varying ways accepted the white man's image of them and survived by building up their own inner defense against it and finding their own ways of expressing their energies and their hopes, their angers and their sorrows.

HAROLD R. ISAACS, 1963

However the white man may have enslaved the Negro's body he did not enslave his soma — his inner stamina, his functions were kept free; and this audacious fact is one of the causes of some white men's envy and fury.   LILLIAN SMITH, 1949

No son of mine will ever shine a white man's shoes.
MAXIE CLEVELAND ROBINSON, SR.

Textbooks now point out that surviving slavery took a skill and stamina that no other race has been called upon to sustain.

ANDREW HACKER, 1992

I was on my way to becoming a master at the game that all African Americans must learn if they wish to preserve their sanity: how to live with reasonable freedom and dignity and yet also avoid insult, disappointment, and conflict rooted in racism.

ARTHUR ASHE, 1993

Racism was not just a black problem. It was America's problem. And until the country solved it, I was not going to let bigotry make me a victim instead of a full human being.

COLIN POWELL, 1995

I tire of wearing blackness as a badge, but I have worn it so long, so well, that I've caught that second wind, that mysterious force that propels me onward and upward. It is this mystic power that anoints my bushy head with a tenacity unpossessed by any other race of man under the heavens, or outside or inside the gates of hell.

CHARLES H. KING, JR., 1983

Fields of play became human proving grounds where blacks had a reasonable shot at disproving the white fantasy about their inferiority. Watching Jackie [Robinson], somehow I decided that I would do that on the sloping grounds of government, philanthropy and journalism, where there are no umpires and where white people cheat and demean blacks every day. I took my fast ball to those fields because Jackie had taught me that a black man need never again submit his psyche to the cruelties of white people's racist fantasies.

ROGER WILKINS, 1982

I have lived in and risen in a white-dominated society and a white-dominated profession, but not by denying my race, not by seeing it as a chain holding me back or an obstacle to be overcome. Others may use my race against me, but I will never use it against myself. My blackness has been a source of pride, strength, and inspiration, and so has my being an American.

I remembered the well-intentioned remarks of some of my white superiors: "Powell, you're the best black lieutenant I've ever known." Thank you, suh. But inside me, I was thinking, if you intend to measure me against only black lieutenants, you are making a mistake. I'm going to show you the best lieutenant in the Army, period.

COLIN POWELL, 1995

To live is to wrestle with despair yet never to allow despair to have the last word.
CORNEL WEST, 1997

Beyond survival lies the potential to perceive more clearly both a reason and the means for further struggle. DERRICK BELL, 1992

One has to view the "new Negro" as . . . the embodiment . . . of healthy strivings that were never smothered, despite all the efforts of an oppressive society. The social blows may bruise, but they do not necessarily crush.
ALEXANDER THOMAS, M.D. 1972

The genius of our black foremothers and forefathers was to create powerful buffers to ward off the nihilistic threat, to equip black folk with cultural armor to beat back the demons of hopelessness, meaninglessness, and lovelessness.
CORNEL WEST, 1993

After centuries of being brainwashed by every symbol and medium of the dominant culture into a sense of their own inferiority and unattractiveness, it was inevitable that Afro-Americans go through a process of psychological liberation that entailed not just the denial of the worthlessness but some emphasis on the positive worth of being Afro-American.　ORLANDO PATTERSON, 1997

By the simple act of survival, the Negro made an inestimable contribution to his posterity and to his native land. . . . He descended into the hell of slavery, was denied books, pencil and paper, was denied the sanctity of marriage — was crucified, in fact, and rose again some three hundred years later in Chicago and Harlem and Atlanta and Washington. *The Negro endured.*

My grandmother and her generation were perhaps the last living witnesses of a religious tradition that surged like billowing flames from the choir lofts and rickety benches of old Baptist and Methodist churches, of a tradition that dared to flesh out that without which religion is a mere Sunday morning game: the fatherhood of God and the brotherhood of man. . . . In the face of overwhelming evidence to the contrary, in the face of lynchings, legalized robbery, institutionalized degradation, they dared to affirm the goodness and the greatness of man.
LERONE BENNETT, JR., 1964

This may strike you as terribly anti-intellectual, or a Rowan version of voodoo, but it is a reality that discerning black people can smell a racist a mile away. Those who have gone through decades of suffering the slings and barbs of bigotry have a sixth sense that tells them who in white America is a friend, who is foe.　CARL T. ROWAN, 1991

As long as hope remains and meaning is preserved, the possibility of overcoming oppression stays alive.
CORNEL WEST, 1993

When you are faced with as many insults, big and small, as black people have to put up with, you learn to laugh or go crazy. Laughing off life's lesser insults helps you to conserve your energies to cope with the bigger ones.
CLARENCE PAGE, 1996

Many white people do not understand how Negroes can laugh at the stupid indignities so often heaped upon them, from high to low, in this American country of ours. . . . Maybe it is this wry laughter that has kept us going all these years, from slavery's denial of the draught of freedom up to the Washington airport's denial of a glass of milk. Maybe it is just a way of saying, "To defeat us you must defeat our laughter." LANGSTON HUGHES, 1948

Oppressed people have a good sense of humor. Think of the Jews. They know how to laugh, and to laugh at themselves! Well, we colored folks are the same way. We colored folks are survivors.

Those rebby types! What do they think, anyway? When we get to the Spirit World, do they think colored people are going to be waiting on their tables, pouring their tea? I think some of them are in for a big surprise. They're going to be pouring tea for *me*. BESSIE DELANY, 1993

In fear and trembling, in blood and suffering, the Negro has retained a certain dark joy — a zest for life, a creative capacity for meeting adversity and transcending it — that is beautiful and meaningful.
LERONE BENNETT, JR., 1964

Had it not been for our art and our culture, when all else was ripped from us, we would never have been able to survive as a people.
HARRY BELAFONTE, 1997

Jim Crow's not law anymore, but it's still in some people's hearts. I don't let it get me, though. I just laugh it off, child. I never let prejudice stop me from what I wanted to do in this life. SADIE DELANY, 1993

Being able to laugh got me through.
TONI MORRISON, 1998

Being American

I was surprised at how patriotic I felt, being the first native-born American winner [in 1993, of the Nobel Prize for Literature] since Steinbeck in 1962. . . . I felt pride that a black and a woman had been recognized in such an international forum.
TONI MORRISON, 1998

The United States of America is your country . . . Some people will tell you it is theirs alone, not yours to share. Don't believe them. . . . You must resist any group that believes it has a proprietary right to guide the ship of state.
ARTHUR ASHE, 1993
To his young daughter

Most African Americans, if given a chance, would have chosen to be "just Americans" ever since the first of us was brought here to Jamestown colony in 1619, a year before the *Mayflower* landed. But that choice has never been left up to us.
CLARENCE PAGE, 1996

Negroes have played a large role in the survival of America. Hundreds of thousands of Negroes, from Bunker Hill to Vietnam, have died for an idea that was not real in their own lives. Has any other people in any other age had such faith and hope — and received so little charity?
LERONE BENNETT, JR., 1964

As children we learned in school about the lowest common denominator; America is about the highest common denominator. That is why Dr. King loved this country. He often spoke about "the glory of America, with all its faults."
VICE PRESIDENT AL GORE, 1998

Segregation and racism had made me loathe aspects of the white South but had left me scarcely less of a patriot. In fact, to me and my family, winning a place on our national team would mark my ultimate triumph over all those people who had opposed my career in the South in the name of segregation.
ARTHUR ASHE, 1993

The Army was living the democratic ideal ahead of the rest of America. Beginning in the fifties, less discrimination, a truer merit system, and leveler playing fields existed inside the gates of our military posts than in any Southern city hall or Northern corporation. The Army, therefore, made it easier for me to love my country, with all its flaws, and to serve her with all my heart.
COLIN POWELL, 1995

Negro men and women signed the Declaration of Independence with the blood of their spirit.
LERONE BENNETT, JR., 1964

The paradox of success

There was a great deal of fuss about being the "first black" . . . The fact that this kind of accomplishment by a black player got so much attention was an indication that we still had so far to go.
ARTHUR ASHE, 1981

The recognized achievements of some Negroes, despite rigid racial barriers, indicate that society by its prejudices may be depriving itself of valuable contributions from many others. It is now doubtful whether America can afford the luxury of such a waste of human resources.
KENNETH B. CLARK, 1963

Black minds and talent have skills to control a spacecraft or scalpel with the same finesse and dexterity with which they control a basketball.
RONALD MCNAIR, 1983

As a celebrity, I encounter few examples of overt racism directed specifically at me. Perhaps I encounter more than I acknowledge, because I never want to dignify ignorant or malicious people by assuming they are fully aware of what they do.
ARTHUR ASHE, 1993

Whatever the dramatic achievements in the lives of individual African Americans, those somehow were not credited to the group in general. Perhaps they should not have been, but they should not have had the opposite effect either. . . . Underneath the fulsome praise was more than a slight suggestion that he or she was the exception that proved the rule.
JOHN HOPE FRANKLIN, 1993

Blacks were routinely denied the recognition of individual talent that is supposed to define the American creed. This history is barely mentioned now that blacks are made by many whites to look as if they duck individual assessment while embracing group privilege.
MICHAEL ERIC DYSON, 1996

America has become comfortable and literally color-blind in its acceptance and adoration of the blacks who entertain, but it is still stubbornly racist in conceding equitable power to blacks in most other arenas. That shouldn't be surprising. The power to entertain is not quite the same as the power to control.
AUDREY EDWARDS / CRAIG K. POLITE, 1992

I had to become so big, so strong, so important that those people and their hatred could never touch me.
SAMMY DAVIS, JR., 1989

An Afro-American music, jazz, is the nation's classical voice, defining, audibly, its entire civilizational style. So powerful and unavoidable is the Afro-American popular influence that it is now common to find people who, while remaining racists in personal relations and attitudes, nonetheless have surrendered their tastes, and much of their viewing and listening time, to Afro-American entertainers, talk-show hosts, and sitcom stars.

ORLANDO PATTERSON, 1997

There is no doubt that white America will accept a black champion, applaud and reward him, as long as there is no "white hope" in sight. But what white America demands in her black champions is a brilliant, powerful body and a dull, bestial mind — a tiger in the ring and a pussycat outside the ring.   ELDRIDGE CLEAVER, 1968

Jackie [Robinson] had to speak out because deep in his heart he knew that no Negro, however famous, however great his contributions, was safe from the poison darts of racial bigotry . . . for in the minds of millions the most accomplished black man would remain "just another Negro," as vulnerable to attitudes of racial superiority as any Mississippi sharecropper.   CARL T. ROWAN, 1960

America does not yet permit Negro artists and intellectuals to wash their hands in the waters of cultural freedom.
LANGSTON HUGHES, 1946

Whites, ready and willing to applaud, even idolize black athletes and entertainers, refuse to hire, or balk at working with, blacks.
DERRICK BELL, 1992

[When Jackie Robinson had to escape from a crowd of fans to catch a plane], it was probably the only day in history that a black man ran from a white mob with love instead of lynching on its mind.   SAM MALTIN, 1960

When I was on that stage . . . it was as though my talent was giving me a pass from their prejudice.
SAMMY DAVIS, JR., 1989

Being a role model

I am just me. . . . I do not and did not and most likely will not ever feel that I have to justify that. I do not have to be a role model, a good person, a credit to the race.   NIKKI GIOVANNI, 1993

Personal success can be no answer. It can no longer be a question of an Anderson, a Carver, a Robinson, or a Robeson. It must be a question of the well-being and opportunities not of a few but for *all* of this great Negro people of which I am a part.   PAUL ROBESON, 1949

How can we elevate Seyi Fayanju, the twelve-year-old black child from Verona, New Jersey, who won the *National Geographic* Geography Bee in a competition of thousands, into a more compelling role model for our children than gangsta rap artists and NBA players?
RANDALL ROBINSON, 1998

All "first blacks" become conditioned to racism and do not allow it to intrude upon their missions or goals. To become a "first black," one had to force himself to accept bias as a way of life, to wink at it, blink at it, and become blind if necessary to its dehumanizing methodology.
CHARLES H. KING, JR., 1983

[Arthur] Ashe had been trained by his father to survive and overcome by making white people comfortable . . . in the Joe Louis tradition . . . never to mock a white opponent or to be photographed with a white woman.
ROBERT LIPSYTE, 1997

Even as race relations in America became increasingly stormy, and I started to feel the attraction of more militant approaches to segregation and racism, I nevertheless saw my Davis Cup appointment as the outstanding honor of my life to that point. Since no black American had ever been on the team, I was now a part of history.
ARTHUR ASHE, 1993

Arthur Ashe was what the white news media and the U.S.T.A. thought the image of a black tennis athlete should be, and they have tried to sell that image even after his death. . . . You don't see young black tennis athletes trying to be like Arthur. Today's role models must be found among the living, not among the dead.
WILLIAM WASHINGTON, 1997

It's not easy to be a martyr in the field of race relations.
JACKIE ROBINSON, 1960

If we're going to have role models — whatever that term may mean — who gets to pick them? Fans, news media, athletes, shoe companies? . . . If Tiger [Woods] and Venus [Williams] don't end up as this decade's Homecoming king and queen, I'll demand a recount. So will Nike.
ROBERT LIPSYTE, 1997

This step is being made . . . by a single individual [Jackie Robinson], by a young man who has already had to undergo racial barbs and humiliations that are sickening to any human being with a heart; by one young man whose wounds you cannot see or share.   BRANCH RICKEY, 1947

The opportunity for one black man to play professional baseball alongside a field full of white men had significance beyond the ballpark. From day one, every step Robinson took seemed tuned to the national imagination, to the dreams — and nightmares — of millions of people. The real burden Robinson bore was that he knew this . . . . In this strange moment it seemed that history could be shaped to the contours of a baseball field.

Robinson's pact with Rickey was to play ball. His pact with himself was to prove beyond any measure that he could not only play with white men, he could play so well that the doors would have to open for others. He was never content merely to fit in; to integrate, he knew that he would always have to be one step ahead.
DAVID FALKNER, 1995

With an earnest zeal, [Jackie Robinson] personified the ritualized angst of racial assimilation.
MICHAEL ANDERSON, 1997

Paul Robeson: Speaking out ahead of his time

We of this less favored race realize that our future lies chiefly in our own hands. . . . But . . . it is necessary that you of the favored race catch a new vision and exemplify in your actions this new American spirit. . . embodying the desire to relieve the manifest distress of your fellows.

Interview, 1935

I believe it would be a good thing for the American Negro to have more consciousness of his African tradition, to be proud of it. Africa has contributed great culture to the world, and will continue to do so.

Speech, 1953

No one has yet explained to my satisfaction what business a black lad from a Mississippi or Georgia share-cropping farm has in Asia shooting down the yellow or brown son of an impoverished rice-farmer.

Here I Stand, 1958

The equal *place* to which we aspire cannot be reached without the equal *rights* we demand, and so the winning of those rights is not a maximum fulfillment but a minimum necessity and we cannot settle for less.

The *power of spirit* that our people have is intangible, but it is a great force that must be unleashed in the struggles of today. A spirit of steadfast determination, exaltation in the face of trials—it is the very soul of our people that has been formed through all the long and weary years of our march toward freedom.

One of the [Congressional] committee members angrily demanded: "Why didn't you stay in Russia?" "Because my father was a slave," I retorted, "and my people died to build this country, and I am going to stay right here and have a part of it, just like you."

The one voice in which we should speak must be the expression of our entire people on the central issue which is all-important to every Negro — our right to be free and equal. On many other issues there are great differences among us, and hence it is not possible for any one person, or any group of people, to presume to speak for us all. . . . A unified leadership of a unified movement means that people of *all* political views — conservatives, liberals, and radicals — must be represented therein.

To achieve the right of full citizenship which is our just demand, we must ever speak and act like free men.

Paul Robeson: Role model for all humanity [1898-1976]

At a time when there seemed to be no hope at all . . . Paul Robeson spoke out . . . for all of us. JAMES BALDWIN, 1965

Paul Robeson is a legendary American, one of the few true Renaissance men of the 20th Century. An actor, singer, scholar, athlete, and political activist, Robeson could dominate a stage or concert hall like the sun radiating its rays across the land on a hot summer day. His rich baritone voice was resonant and melodic. He enraptured his audiences with his talent — despite the color of his skin.

Had Robeson been born white, or had he been born in a more tolerant era, every school child would speak his name along with Muhammad Ali's and Martin Luther King's. But . . . he was doomed to be stifled by the climate of his times. . . . His successes . . . were ultimately overshadowed by heartache and rejection, the result of a society which would not tolerate a Black man who spoke his mind.

ROB EDELMAN, 1979

The man

Before King dreamed, before Thurgood Marshall petitioned and Sidney Poitier emoted, before the big breakthroughs in Hollywood and Washington, before the Jim Crow signs came down and before the civil rights banners went up, before Spike Lee, before Denzel [Washington], before Sam Jackson and Jesse Jackson, there was Paul Robeson. One of the most phenomenally gifted men ever born in America . . . he lived one of the most extraordinary stories of the century . . . When he died . . . even his critics and detractors conceded that he was one of the immortals.

LERONE BENNETT, JR., 1998

His has been appropriately called democracy's most powerful voice. Nature endowed him with a magnificent talent, housed it in a . . . most attractive frame; provided a winsome and congenial personality to go along with it; instilled in him a quality of courage in direct ratio to his enormous physique; and topped it off by saturating this extraordinary man with boundless love for his fellows and an uncompromising hatred of injustice and oppression in all their ugly forms. He, on his part, accepted these gifts as tools with which to work. . . . He has probably personally addressed, in speech and in song, without the aid of television, more people on the earth, than any other living human being. HOPE R. STEVENS, 1965

Paul was a man and a half, and we have no category, even now, to hold the size of him. . . . Athletic champion, yes; Phi Beta Kappa scholar, singer, actor, spokesman, activist, leader — yes! Africanist, socialist, black Nationalist — all that, too, but something more, something new, something different. . . . He had studied many life styles till they became his by second nature, was himself transfigured by what he learned, and became by *accident* what socialist societies are meant to produce by design.   OSSIE DAVIS, 1971

To tell of the achievements, the successes and the experiences of Paul Robeson would be to relate the history of most of the first half of this century. . . . Love for people, a passion for justice and a yearning for freedom. That is the Paul Robeson that no power on earth can conceal. . . . How tragic for this present generation of our youth to be denied his participation in their lives! Not only the magnificence of his art, but also the genius of his mind — and for black youth in particular. What a model for this and every generation to aspire to!   GEORGE W. CROCKETT, 1973

He is one of the few of whom I would say that they have greatness. . . . I despair of ever putting into convincing words my notion of this quality in him. I can say only that by what he does, thinks and is, by his unassailable dignity, and his serene, incorruptible simplicity, Paul Robeson strikes me as having been made out of the original stuff of the world. In this sense he is coeval with Adam and the redwood trees of California. He is a fresh act, a fresh gesture, a fresh effort of creation.
ALEXANDER WOOLLCOTT, 1934

The tallest tree in our forest has fallen. Along with the countless persons here and around the world who mourn his loss, I think Nature herself must feel that with the passing of Paul Robeson something uniquely wonderful has departed from the earth. . . . A whole generation must be startled to learn now that such a person actually existed in their lifetime — a modern-day black American with the manifold talents of a Renaissance man!
LLOYD L. BROWN, 1976

The remarkably wonderful thing about the principles for which Paul Robeson stood during his lifetime is that they remain relevant and even urgent today. . . . Very few . . . have the courage to speak out in support of unpopular causes when the stakes are high and the risks are many. In taking his stand, Robeson was such a person; and although his stands caused him much anguish and even pain and physical suffering, he saw no alternative. . . . It was his failure to be a narrow-minded nationalist that led many of his fellow Americans to turn against him. But it was this world view that placed him ahead of his time.
JOHN HOPE FRANKLIN, 1998

The heritage

His father had been a slave in North Carolina, and when, afterwards, a Methodist preacher holding revivalist meetings, he used to sing the songs of the slave days, the boy Paul learned them and carried them about, sunk deep in his heart. Out of them now he is making a great international reputation.
HANNEN SWAFFER, 1929

The scholar / athlete

When the 1917 football season ended, Paul Robeson was considered by many experts to be the best football player in America. . . . Walter Camp, who was often referred to as the father of American football, judged the black star to be the all-time best at his position. . . . In his third year he added baseball and track. . . . And then . . . Robey also tried out for and won a place on the varsity debating team. 　　　　　　LLOYD L. BROWN, 1997

[In 1919] in recognition of his excellence in class and on campus, the president of [Rutgers University] chose him as commencement orator. Robeson selected as his title, "Our New Idealism." . . . His speech was a triumph — epochal, as it were, in the history of the college. 　　　　　　J. A. ROGERS, 1947

The singer

I have heard all the great singers of our time. No voice has moved me so profoundly with so many passions of thought and emotion. . . . We laughed and wept. He broke our hearts with beauty.
　　　　　　JAMES DOUGLAS, 1928

He is the finest musical instrument wrought by nature in our time.
　　　　　　ALEXANDER WOOLLCOTT, 1934

As a musician he is known as a singer of Negro song — pieces in the vernacular. He himself says, "I sing the Negro songs because they suit my voice and suit me."
　　　　　　MAUD CUNEY-HARE, 1936

His rendition of English, Hebrew, Mexican, Russian and German folk songs, often sung both in the original tongue and in English, shows the same understanding and deep sincerity that make him the most famous male singer of Negro spirituals of his day.
　　　　　　CURRENT BIOGRAPHY, 1941

Paul sang the songs of freedom, of love, of gaiety, of hope, with a new meaning for all oppressed and dispossessed people — but particularly for black people. The songs of protest and solace that the black people of America had composed and sung to noteless music for over three centuries, he dignifed and glorified by presenting them with pride and confidence everywhere he went.
　　　　　　HOPE R. STEVENS, 1965

Paul Robeson became the voice of the cultural heritage, not only of the Afro-American people, but of the entire international working class. So far as this country is concerned, we may consider him the father of the American political song of the contemporary era. 　　　PHILIP S. FONER, 1978

The actor

Mr. Robeson's Ebon Othello [in London] is as sturdy as an oak, deep-rooted in its elemental passion and many branched in its early tenderness, a superb giant of the woods for the great hurricane of tragedy to whisper through, then rage open, then break. One thinks of a tree because the greatness is of nature, not of art.
　　　　　　IVOR BROWN, 1930

[Robeson] gave a portrayal of great resonance, vitality, and fluency, and one surpassing any Othello within my experience. He brings majesty and power to the role, as well as pathos and terror.

WARD MOREHOUSE, 1943

Robeson received one of the most prolonged and wildest ovations in the history of the New York theatre. LIFE MAGAZINE, 1943

The activist

In honoring you today, we do not . . . express our enthusiasm for your histrionic and musical achievements alone. We honor you chiefly as a man — a man of tremendous stature, energy and physical dexterity; a man of brilliant mind, a man whose sensitive spirit makes possible your penetrating interpretations; and a man who, above all else, travels across the world as an example of the humanity and the greatness of our democratic heritage. W. H. COWLEY, 1940
President, Hamilton College, on conferring honorary degree of Doctor of Humane Letters

Never reticent about his social outlook, Mr. Robeson has often expressed it not only in the choice of some of his program numbers . . . but also in his remarks from the platform introducing these songs. . . . "I want to use my singing for direct political action against fascism in America," he explained to reporters. "I feel that singing pretty songs is not enough." JULIUS BLOOM, 1947

For two generations of Americans, Paul Robeson represented the entire Negro people of this country. He was a spectacular hero who seemed to have been born lucky. . . . He might have kept quiet as so many other Negro celebrities have done; he might have taken it easier, and kept his friends happy, but he couldn't. . . . We salute more than a man, we salute a cause. We salute the dreams and aspirations and the hopes of an oppressed people whether they be in Selma, Alabama, in Jackson, Mississippi, or in Vietnam.

JOHN LEWIS, 1965

He spoke and lived black pride before it became politically acceptable in the white community; Paul Robeson is a model of black political activism. . . . He transcended his time, his race, and his own person to join that select group of souls who speak for all humanity. EDWARD J. BLOUSTEIN, 1972

If ever a man placed himself on the altar of sacrifice for his people, that man was Paul Robeson. In the climate in which he refused to bend the knee to the tyrants of thought-control and paid the price therefor, others less rigid or less strong — in conformity or by compromise — went on to riches and approval. . . . After the names and the deeds of the pygmies who in their pomp and circumstance attempted to detract and to defame him have long been forgotten — this moral giant of our time will live in the hearts of his people and of the fighters for freedom yet unborn, and his voice can never be stilled.

HOPE R. STEVENS, 1965

WHOSE PROBLEM?
Racism and society

Am I an American?
I'm — just — an
Irish, Negro, Jewish, Italian,
French and English, Spanish, Russian,
Chinese, Polish, Scotch, Hungarian,
Litvak, Swedish, Finnish, Canadian,
Greek and Turk, and Czech
and double-Czech American.
And that ain't all,
I was baptized
Baptist, Methodist, Congregationalist,
Lutheran, Atheist, Roman Catholic,
Orthodox Jewish, Presbyterian,
Seventh-Day Adventist, Mormon, Quaker,
Christian Scientist
— and lots more!

JOHN LATOUCHE, 1940

SECTARIAN BITTERNESS.

White privilege

> Every white person who is not too caught up in his or her own sense of righteous victimization knows that white skin still affords certain privileges in our color-coded society.
> CLARENCE PAGE, 1996

> Malcolm [X] knew that every white man in America profits directly or indirectly from his position vis-à-vis Negroes, profits from racism even though he does not practice it or believe it.
> OSSIE DAVIS, 1965

> No white American, including those who insist that opportunities exist for persons of every race, would change places with even the most successful black American.
> ANDREW HACKER, 1992

We have long since grown accustomed to thinking of Blacks as being "racially disadvantaged." Rarely, however, do we refer to Whites as "racially *ad*vantaged," even though that is an equally apt characterization of the existing inequality.
HARLON L. DALTON, 1995

As a white person, I realized I had been taught about racism as something which puts others at a disadvantage, but had been taught not to see one of its corollary aspects, white privilege, which puts me at an advantage.

Many, perhaps most, of our white students in the United States think that racism doesn't affect them because they are not people of color; they do not see "whiteness" as a racial identity.

In my class and place, I did not recognize myself as a racist because I was taught to see racism only in individual acts of meanness by members of my group, never in invisible systems conferring unsought racial dominance on my group from birth.
PEGGY MCINTOSH, 1988

Centuries of discrimination had significantly diminished the economic competition encountered by whites. Loud proclamations of white self-sufficiency ignored a more subtle truth: The incalculable value of being white in America rested to a large extent on the calculable disadvantage of being black.
TOM WICKER, 1996

Privilege is least apparent to those who have it.
CLARENCE PAGE, 1996

Whiteness in a racist, corporate-controlled society is like having the image of an American Express Card . . . stamped on one's face: immediately you are "universally accepted."
MANNING MARABLE, 1997

In settings where Whites dominate, being White is not noteworthy. It is like the tick of a familiar clock, part of the easily tuned-out background noise.
HARLON L. DALTON, 1995

When whites are forced to look honestly upon the objective proof of their deeds, the cement of mendacity holding white society together swiftly disintegrates.
ELDRIDGE CLEAVER, 1968

I don't think most whites understand what it is to be black in the United States today. They don't even have a clue. They blame the blacks to a large degree for their own problems. . . . As a white, I can tell you that whites have a lot to do to make it a fair game.
DOUGLAS MASSEY, 1992

In our culture, whiteness is rarely marked in the indicative there! there! sense of my bracketed blackness. And the majoritarian privilege of never noticing themselves was the beginning of an imbalance from which so much, so much else flowed.
PATRICIA WILLIAMS, 1997

This is a racist nation. I am a racist and you are a racist because we've had the advantage from the day we were born. We may not be bigots. . . But I'm still a racist because my tribe still has the power and seems determined to hang onto it.
WILL D. CAMPBELL, 1992

Nothing that we do is qualified, limited, discredited or acclaimed simply because of our racial background. We don't have to represent our race, and nothing we do is judged as a credit to our race, or as confirmation of its shortcomings or inferiority.
PAUL KIVEL, 1993

I am afraid the nerve of some white folks has gone to their heads and affected their brains so that they can't think right — only white — which is too bad, because this is *our* world, too, so they had better get over that.
LANGSTON HUGHES, 1945

We must take whiteness itself and hold it up to the light and see that it is a color too.
PAUL KIVEL, 1993

A shared destiny . . .

Many of our white brothers . . . have come to realize that their destiny is tied up with our destiny and they have come to realize that their freedom is inextricably bound to our freedom.
MARTIN LUTHER KING, JR.
(Dream) 1963

There are no winners and losers in the battle against racism. Its defeat is not a victory for one particular group, but for society as a whole, and for us all as human beings.
PROJECT HIP-HOP, 1997

We must be together. This is not a matter of doing something "for" blacks or "for" whites; it is a matter of making American society viable in the future.
THOMAS F. PETTIGREW, 1971

Actively we have woven ourselves with the very warp and woof of this nation — we have fought their battles, shared their sorrow, mingled our blood with theirs, and generation after generation have pleaded with a headstrong, careless people to despise not justice, mercy, and truth, lest the nation be smitten with a curse. Our song, our toil, our cheer, and warning have been given to this nation in blood-brotherhood.
W.E.B. DU BOIS, 1903

Black America is called upon to stand as the protagonist of tolerance, of fair play, of justice, and of good will. Until white America heeds, we shall never let its conscience sleep. For the responsibility for the outcome is not ours alone. White America cannot save itself if it prevents us from being saved.
JAMES WELDON JOHNSON, 1934

The relationship between American society and the Negro problem is not one-sided. The entire structure of American society is itself greatly conditioned by the presence of the thirteen million Negro citizens.

The Negro problem is not only America's greatest failure but also America's incomparably great opportunity for the future. If America should follow its own deepest convictions, its well-being at home would be increased directly. . . . America can demonstrate that justice, equality and cooperation are possible between white and colored people.
GUNNAR MYRDAL, 1942

Would America have been America without her Negro people?
W.E.B. DU BOIS, 1903

Just as most Negroes still believe that the ultimate solution for us is in America, I am firmly convinced that the ultimate salvation of America is the Negro.
JOHN OLIVER KILLENS, 1964

The question of the Negro's place in America, which for a long time could actually be kicked around as a serious question, has been decisively resolved: he is here to stay.
ELDRIDGE CLEAVER, 1968

If we were to take joint responsibility for cleaning up the racial mess, we could search for creative solutions that expand opportunities for everyone. . . . In a very real sense Black liberation holds the promise of White liberation as well.
HARLON L. DALTON, 1995

I think it is naive in the extreme to assert that there is no persistent vulnerability to prejudice — rooted in human nature, prejudice based on race and ethnicity — and other characteristics as well. . . . Yet, in our society, when we have this increasing diversity, we have a community value, a national interest in helping to overcome this inherent vulnerability.
VICE PRESIDENT AL GORE, 1997

Both Northerners and Southerners often make the mistake of assuming that the race situation is an exclusively Southern problem. Actually, it is an American problem. While it has different aspects in the North and in the South, anything that is done about it, good or bad, has national repercussions; and the individual citizen is involved, not as a Northerner or Southerner, but as an American.
MARGARET HALSEY, 1946

The choice was not alone between fairness and unfairness to an oppressed people, but also between wholeness and division in the family of man. It was between integration and disintegration in our very hearts, between love and hate — between the highest and the lowest values I knew.
SARAH PATTON BOYLE, 1962

We are caught in an inescapable network of mutuality, tied in a single garment of destiny. Whatever affects one directly affects all indirectly. Never again can we afford to live with the narrow, provincial "outside agitator" idea. Anyone who lives in the United States can never be considered an outsider anywhere in this country.
MARTIN LUTHER KING, JR., (Letter) 1963

Both black and white are trapped by race.
DOUGLAS MASSEY, 1992

Racism always involves an injustice committed by one person or group against another person or group for reasons of race, color, religion or political ideology. It is fatal in the end because it always works to damage *both* groups.
JOHN HOWARD GRIFFIN, 1977

If we do not want a black Ireland here, if we do not want our cities divided into mutually hostile casbahs, if we do not want the Negro rebellion to become a real revolution, then we must dare to flesh out the words we profess.
LERONE BENNETT, JR., 1964

The integration of the Negro into American society is one of the most exciting challenges to self-development and self-mastery that any nation of people ever faced.
MARGARET HALSEY, 1946

Too many African-American leaders fail to grasp — as Martin Luther King, Jr., did — that their task is not simply to lead blacks but to lead blacks and whites. . . . We have had too few who spoke *from* the souls of black folk while speaking *to* the souls of us all.
CHRISTOPHER EDLEY, JR., 1996

We can embrace our diversity, find strength in it, and prosper together, or we can focus on our differences and try to restrict access to resources by members of ethnic and racial groups different from ours and limit prosperity for all.
ANDREW YOUNG, 1996

We, the black and white, deeply need each other here if we are really to become a nation — if we are really, that is, to achieve our identity, our maturity, as men and women. To create one nation has proved to be a hideously difficult task; there is certainly no need now to create two, one black and one white.
JAMES BALDWIN, 1963

When our politicians appeal to our greed, our selfishness, and our fear, we have the power to say to them, "We are better than that." . . . This is the meaning that informs our defense of affirmative action. None of us is free until all of us are free.
CHARLES R. LAWRENCE III / MARI J. MATSUDA, 1997

The long noble struggle for civil rights . . . was a struggle to free white people, too.
PRESIDENT BILL CLINTON, (June 14) 1997

. . . or a divided one

There is nothing inherently wrong with being aware of color . . . It is only when character is attached to color, when ability is measured by color, when privilege is tied to color, and a whole galaxy of factors that spell the difference between success and failure in our society are tied to color . . . that it becomes a deadly, dreadful, denigrating factor among us all . . . that we have two nations, black and white, separate, hostile, unequal.

JOHN HOPE FRANKLIN, 1993

After years of enduring America at home and watching her abroad, I am convinced that I will die in a society as racially divided as the one into which I was born more than a half century ago. This no longer appears to concern white Americans.

We are, in America, now sealed off from each other in well-defended racial camps with negligible intergroup knowledge or communication. . . . Better we face the painful problem now than the conflagration looming ahead.

RANDALL ROBINSON, 1998

The many sharp differences between the races, expressed along hardened political and social battle lines, may be precursors for an escalating racial conflict and, ultimately, conflagration. This process is already at work, and accelerating. . . . The peril must be an impetus for self-conscious projects to build bridges among communities.

CHRISTOPHER EDLEY, JR., 1996

If we say, as we do, that no one in this country intends for racism to lead to genocide, the effects of racism are genocidal, regardless of our intentions.

JOHN HOWARD GRIFFIN, 1977

We must acknowledge that as a people — *E Pluribus Unum* — we are on a slippery slope toward economic strife, social turmoil, and cultural chaos. If we go down, we go down together.

CORNEL WEST, 1993

When cities go up in smoke . . . we stop and say we have to do something about it. . . . Cities will burn until we decide, once and for all, to root out the cause of such self-immolation.

CHARLES R. LAWRENCE III / MARI J. MATSUDA, 1997

The problem of the twentieth century is the problem of civilizing white people.
NIKKI GIOVANNI, 1993

Turn now and look at black America. We are not only separated by geographical and discriminatory containment, but also isolated in spirit. We have become a separate people — both in philosophy and in experience. That black experience is unknown to white America.

CHARLES H. KING, JR., 1983

Real community is based on reciprocity of emotion and relation between individuals sharing a common vision of the possibilities and potentialities of man. The basic fact of race relations in America is that white people and Negroes do not belong to the same community.

Ten years from now or twenty years from now, when Negroes comprise from one-third to more than one-half of the population of our major cities, a bill is coming due. Sooner or later, in a good season or a bad season, the Commonwealth is going to have to decide between the American idea or Fascism.

LERONE BENNETT, JR., 1964

A huge racial chasm remains, and there are few signs that the coming century will see it closed. A century and a quarter after slavery, white America continues to ask of its black citizens an extra patience and perseverance that whites have never required of themselves. So the question for white America is essentially moral: is it right to impose on members of an entire race a lesser start in life, and then to expect from them a degree of resolution that has never been demanded from your own race?

ANDREW HACKER, 1992

If we, who can scarcely be considered a white nation, persist in thinking of ourselves as one, we condemn ourselves, with the truly white nations, to sterility and decay.

The Negroes of this country may never be able to rise to power, but they are very well placed indeed to precipitate chaos and ring down the curtain on the American dream.

JAMES BALDWIN, 1963

For me, the agony of observing and living the contemporary problem of race in America is just this: to hold simultaneously the fear of war and the dream of community.

CHRISTOPHER EDLEY, JR., 1996

The fault line of race is the paramount factor in keeping us from realizing our full potential as a people.
WILLIAM F. WINTER, 1997

Integration . . .

True integration, unlike assimilation, is a two-way street. It involves *cultural sharing*, a genuine respect and interest in difference, not cultural submergence by one party to please another.

Instead of the melting pot metaphor, I prefer the mulligan stew. . . . Everything went into the pot and was stirred up, but the pieces didn't melt.
CLARENCE PAGE, 1996

On the one hand, how do we maintain the rituals, the mother tongues, the intimacies that reinforce the boundaries of what keeps us sane? On the other, how do we remain open to the possibility that my son may want to marry your daughter?
PATRICIA WILLIAMS, 1997

This is what Negroes have meant and mean now by integration. It simply means being included in everything that everybody is included in. The rest would be up to the free interplay of society, group, and individual.
HAROLD R. ISAACS, 1963

For genuine integration to exist, the two races must be of equal status and have equal access to resources . . . "Racial integration" . . . is not to be confused with mere desegregation or with the assimilation of black Americans into so-called "white American standards" — two misinterpretations common in the mass media. There is, of course, precious little racial integration fitting this rigorous definition in the United States today.
THOMAS F. PETTIGREW, 1971

The solution may be a long way off, but I think there is more understanding between white kids and black kids than there was thirty years ago. The hope is that, slowly, America, the melting pot that accepted immigrants like my family, can do the same thing for the people who were already here.
FRED WERNER, 1992

In view of the forces at work in the situation, the integration of the Negro American into American society will, when it is finally accomplished, be one of the greatest monuments to the human spirit in all of history.
MARGARET HALSEY, 1946

The attainment of a viable, democratic nation . . . requires extensive racial integration in all realms of life.
THOMAS F. PETTIGREW, 1971

On the one hand, integration is true intergroup, interpersonal living. On the other hand, it is the mutual sharing of power. I cannot see how the Negro will be totally liberated from the crushing weight of poor education, squalid housing and economic strangulation until he is integrated, with power, into every level of American life. MARTIN LUTHER KING, JR., 1967

You will never get the American white man to accept the so-called Negro as an integrated part of his society until the image of the Negro the white man has is changed, and until the image the Negro has of himself is also changed. MALCOLM X, 1962

A certain despair rises . . . not only among youthful newcomers but . . . in older men weary of having to continue a struggle that they thought, for a brief time in the 1950's, might really be coming to an end at last. . . . One comes upon the feeling that effective integration for Negroes in the American society is unlikely, impossible, or even no longer desirable. HAROLD R. ISAACS, 1963

As the relations between the previously segregated groups change, becoming objectively better for Afro-Americans, they will be experienced by Afro-Americans as getting much worse even as they are genuinely seen by Euro-Americans to be improving. Both perceptions will be correct.

If the integration of two groups legally and socially separated for more than 350 years does not produce friction, it is the surest sign that no meaningful change has taken place. ORLANDO PATTERSON, 1997

Historical events become convenient excuses for those who want to drive people apart instead of bringing them together.

One of the problems . . . is that you can win a lot of arguments, yet you look in people's eyes and you see that you haven't changed them. There is something still being held back, some core you haven't touched.
PRESIDENT BILL CLINTON
(Spring) 1998

Dealing with race needn't be like going to an old-fashioned dentist.
HARLON L. DALTON, 1995

How can one respect, let alone adopt, the values of a people who do not, on any level whatever, live the way they say they do, or the way they say they should? . . . I am far from convinced that being released from the African witch doctor was worthwhile if I am now — in order to support the moral contradictions and the spiritual aridity of my life — expected to become dependent on the American psychiatrist. It is a bargain I refuse.

JAMES BALDWIN, 1963

This word "integration" has millions of white people confused, and angry, believing wrongly that the black masses want to live mixed up with the white man.   MALCOLM X, 1965

Life's piano can only produce the melodies of brotherhood when it is recognized that the black keys are as basic, necessary and beautiful as the white keys. The Negro, through self-acceptance and self-appreciation, will one day cause white America to see that integration is not an obstacle, but an opportunity to participate in the beauty of diversity.

A vigorous enforcement of civil rights will bring an end to segregated public facilities, but it cannot bring an end to fears, prejudice, pride and irrationality, which are the barriers to a truly integrated society.

MARTIN LUTHER KING, JR.
1967

Let us . . . not think of our movement as one that seeks to integrate the Negro into all the existing values of American society. Let us be those creative dissenters who will call our beloved nation to a higher destiny, to a new plateau of compassion, to a more noble expression of humaneness.   MARTIN LUTHER KING, JR., 1967

Integration and transformation: these two themes are at the heart of the rebellion which holds enormous possibilities for all Americans. For if the rebellion fulfills itself it will stimulate our creativity which only comes from diversity; it will relieve the drab sameness of our middle-class minds and our middle-class neighborhoods; it will give us an America more concerned about the claims of human personality and less concerned about color and machines.

LERONE BENNETT, JR., 1964

Integration is not about rubbing shoulders with whites; it's about becoming engineers.
ANDREW YOUNG, 1996

Subcultures often have much to teach the mainstream. Until Americans are willing to show a little more genuine curiosity about the joys and pains of one another's ethnic and racial experiences, we will continue to build walls between one another and true integration will continue to be nothing more than an elusive dream.

CLARENCE PAGE, 1996

We are not fighting for the right to be like you. We respect ourselves too much for that. When we fight for freedom, we mean freedom for us to be black, or brown, and you to be white and yet live together in a free and equal society. This is the only way that integration can mean dignity for both of us.

JOHN OLIVER KILLENS, 1964

If some measure of successful integration does finally offer the Negro a more tolerable life as an *American* — where will it leave him as *Negro*? . . . The conquest of civil rights carries us toward those vague and shadowy places where all the new questions about the future of the Negro group identity wait for us.

HAROLD R. ISAACS, 1963

At the price of becoming pseudowhites, we have been admitted in small numbers as probationary members of American society. "Integration" on those terms was an idea that was foredoomed to be rejected by the mass of black Americans. . . . It does not close or even appreciably narrow the gulf between them and the greater society.

SHIRLEY CHISHOLM, 1970

It will do black Americans absolutely no good to be politically and economically enfranchised into a system that systematically denies human values.

SHIRLEY CHISHOLM, 1970

Of course, by now everyone has heard the story of the Southern senator in Washington who became unduly friendly toward a colored lady typist in one of the government offices. When his Dixie cronies reproached him about it, he said, "But I don't want to go to school with her. I just want to have a date."

LANGSTON HUGHES, 1958

In practice, there is nothing especially dramatic in people getting along well together.
MARGARET HALSEY, 1946

. . . or resegregation

Before we throw around the word "resegregate," the campuses must first desegregate.

There are two sets of reasons for self-segregation. One is to be with people who are like you. The other is to get away from people who are not like you.

CLARENCE PAGE, 1996

The problem of identity and image is the key to why more blacks are seeking black institutions for their educational growth.

CHARLES H. KING, JR., 1983

The thought that repeatedly haunts me as I travel the nation's campuses is that the South did indeed finally win the moral battle over integration, for no group of people now seems more committed to segregation than Afro-American students and young professionals. The motto now seems to be an in-your-face "separate yes, but make damn sure it's equal, by affirmative action or any other means."

ORLANDO PATTERSON, 1997

Working against the integrationist impulse is the affinity impulse, the desire to spend time with those who share your background and values. You miss the old familiar. . . At the roots of resegregation are a set of *parallel realities*, each defined by decidedly different ways of looking at the world.

The self-segregation we see today may be the early vision of a new, pluralistic, multicultural century that will see blacks become a part of the economic and political mainstream but . . . maintain their cultural integrity and identity.

White people are quick to notice whenever black people are getting tribal. They are slow to notice that white people are still tribal, too. . . . Black students sitting with one another is called "self-segregating" or "balkanizing." White students sitting together is called "normal." If self-segregation is not a virtue, it also must be remembered that, alas, students of color didn't invent it.

CLARENCE PAGE, 1996

To prescribe more separation . . . is like getting drunk again to cure a hangover.
THOMAS F. PETTIGREW, 1971

That large and unmeasured number who are now banging on the doors of black institutions are echoing a new song to whites who now are attempting to integrate them into their settings: "When you could, you wouldn't; now you want to, but you can't." It is, in essence, a farewell to the white plantation.

CHARLES H. KING, JR., 1983

> If many black students choose predominantly black schools, it may be a very rational choice. . . . to avoid the racism and alienation they may encounter at largely white campuses.
> ANDREW HACKER, 1992

In 1954, the Supreme Court outlawed officially segregated schools on the ground that they generated in black students "a feeling of inferiority as to their status in the community." Now, a generation later, it is being argued that blacks who go to schools with predominantly white enrollments can end up with the same inferior feelings. There is no inconsistency here. Today, the people proposing separate schools want those who enroll to sign up voluntarily. And, at least as important, these schools should be under black control.   ANDREW HACKER, 1992

> Persisting segregation is partly — and for most middle-class Afro-Americans, largely — a voluntary phenomenon. As a strong believer in integration, I personally find this fact discouraging, but one simply has to face up to it.
> ORLANDO PATTERSON, 1997

Separatism is not a practical alternative in a country with so much diversity. . . . To actually withdraw, to pretend that you can hold the country together while being in separate enclaves, is an illusion. All you have to do is look around the world to see what happens when people have tried that.   PRESIDENT BILL CLINTON, (Spring) 1998

> Segregation is no longer the law, but too often, separation is still the rule. . . . The alternative to integration is not isolation or a new separate but equal, it is disintegration.
> PRESIDENT BILL CLINTON
> (September 25) 1997

We are a nation of unlimited opportunity *and* serious unsolved social ills; and we are all in it together. Racial resegregation can only lead to social disintegration. Far better to resume the dream of Martin Luther King, Jr.: to build a nation where whites and blacks sit side by side at the table of brotherhood.   COLIN POWELL, 1995

The nation's binge of *apartheid* must not be exacerbated but alleviated.
THOMAS F. PETTIGREW, 1971

The limits of law

Intelligent propaganda, legal enactment and reasoned action must attack the conditioned reflexes of race hate and change them.
W.E.B. DU BOIS, 1940

The enforcement of the law is itself a form of peaceful persuasion. But the law needs help. . . . In the end, for laws to be obeyed, men must believe they are right.
MARTIN LUTHER KING, JR. 1958

Prejudices are not likely to be reduced by laws which, in the manner of their passing, arouse other prejudices. GORDON ALLPORT, 1954

We need to appreciate the importance of legislation, judicial decisions, and executive orders . . . Without them it is not possible for individuals or groups of individuals, however dedicated, to make a good-faith and successful effort to eliminate the color line.
JOHN HOPE FRANKLIN, 1993

The civil rights measures of the 1960's engraved solemn rights in the legal literature. But after writing piecemeal and incomplete legislation and proclaiming its historic importance in magnificent prose, the American Government left the Negro to make the unworkable work.

Throughout our history, laws affirming Negro rights have consistently been circumvented . . . Laws that affect the whole population — draft laws, income-tax laws, traffic laws — manage to work even though they may be unpopular; but laws passed for the Negro's benefit are so widely unenforced that it is a mockery to call them laws.
MARTIN LUTHER KING, JR., 1967

America has the laws and the material resources it takes to insure justice for all its people. What it lacks is the heart, the humanity, the Christian love that it would take.

In spite of all the passion, the sacrifices, and the idealism that the civil rights movement called forth, it left little behind it but some new laws that have yet to be really enforced.
SHIRLEY CHISHOLM, 1970

There is a tragic gulf between civil rights laws passed and civil rights laws implemented.
MARTIN LUTHER KING, JR., 1967

The hard-won civil rights legislation of the 1960s, which I benefited from, was fought for . . . over the opposition of those hiding behind transparent arguments of "states' rights" and "property rights."

COLIN POWELL, 1995

While state and local laws requiring segregation have been nullified, the goal of racial integration has not been achieved.

ANDREW HACKER, 1992

We were all, as it turns out, extremely naive about the capacity of a legal revolution to create a political and cultural revolution . . . [Discrimination] was too embedded in the bones and blood of the body politic. It was too much in the heads of too many parents raising too many children to have gone away simply because laws were passed.

IRA GLASSER, 1994

Antidiscrimination laws tell us what not to do and how to behave under specified formal circumstances. They do not, and cannot, dictate how we are to interact in everyday encounters.   ORLANDO PATTERSON, 1997

America has traveled and is still traveling a long, hard road . . . littered with . . . persistent intolerance and bigotry. However, our progress as a nation has been marked by a succession of civil rights laws, standposts that rise above political party and endure as lasting, bipartisan achievements. . . . Without proper enforcement, these laws are merely empty promises.   BILL LANN LEE, 1997

Basing our self-esteem on the ability to look down on others is not the American way. . . . We have torn down the barriers in our laws. Now we must break down the barriers in our lives, our minds, and our hearts.

PRESIDENT BILL CLINTON, (June 14) 1997

What is integration when the law says yes, but the police and howling mobs say no?
ROBERT F. WILLIAMS, 1964

The economic gap

> Most Americans have never seen the ignorance, degradation, hunger, sickness, and futility in which many other Americans live. Until a problem reaches their doorsteps, they're not going to understand.
> SHIRLEY CHISHOLM, 1970

> We must accent the best of each other even as we point out the vicious effects of our racial divide and the pernicious consequences of our maldistribution of wealth and power.
> CORNEL WEST, 1994

> To put it bluntly, beneath the record-breaking stock markets on Wall Street and bipartisan budget-balancing deals in the White House lurk ominous clouds of despair across the nation.
> CORNEL WEST, 1997

The pattern of racial disparities in economic and social conditions remains painfully stark. This is not the America we want; the most unrepentant apologist for the status quo cannot dress it up to make an appealing portrait of American justice.   CHRISTOPHER EDLEY, JR., 1996

The present emphasis on studying the poor and the blacks implies that these are the "problem" groups. The real problem resides in the haves rather than the have nots. What stands in the way of social advance is resistance to change on the part of the rich and powerful, their reluctance to give up even a tiny fraction of their privileges.
ALEXANDER THOMAS, M.D., 1972

When enough Americans realize how rotten are the fruits of our policy of "benign neglect," how costly our prejudice is both in dollars and in human misery, the demand for change will be made — not for the sake of minority people but for the sake of us all.
JOHN HOWARD GRIFFIN, 1977

Immigrants from Africa, Asia and the Pacific, Central and Latin America and the Caribbean, have made the "minority" population increasingly diverse. . . . The politics of divide and rule set one group against another, and encourage them to fight for the ever smaller pieces of the American pie reserved for people who are neither white, nor well off.   PROJECT HIP-HOP, 1997

To be a poor man is hard, but to be a poor race in a land of dollars is the very bottom of hardships.
W.E.B. DU BOIS, 1903

The problem of the great majority of the Afro-American poor is the problem of income inequality. In a land of extraordinary abundance, the top fifth greedily takes so much that the bottom fifth, even working two jobs, sinks deeper and deeper into poverty.

ORLANDO PATTERSON, 1997

My conservative friends seem to have a Marxist worldview that the economy is a fixed pie, that in order for the poor to get more, the rich must get less. But . . . the more people included in the economy, the more growth and the larger one's slice becomes. In an economy that is producing equitable growth, wealthier citizens find they may have a smaller percentage of a much larger pie, but the result is greater wealth all around.

Federal programs that would alleviate conditions for the most needy in our society . . . were labeled "creeping socialism." The federal government should not "interfere" with the free enterprise system, it was said. Yet we noted that leaders of the free enterprise system did not hesitate to turn to the federal government when they need help. "Socialism" was just fine when it was socialism for the rich.

What had begun as a movement for racial equality had evolved until Martin [Luther King] could no longer ignore the role that war and poverty played . . . Only when we removed the first layer of segregation did we see clearly the cancer of poverty eating away at the hope and strength of black people in America. Segregation nourished that cancer, but the elimination of segregation could not eradicate it. . . . By attacking poverty, Martin was calling into question fundamental patterns of American life.

ANDREW YOUNG, 1996

One must question the values of a society that tolerates the kind of poverty that exists in the United States.

ANDREW YOUNG, 1996

Where we had been two Americas, whites and blacks, we were soon to become three, the whites, the blacks who would now rise, and finally the millions of bottom-mired blacks who could not.

RANDALL ROBINSON, 1998

The challenge remains to harness the power of prosperity and turn it to overcoming poverty and despair. . . . To continue to ignore the less fortunate among us will place the nation in peril.

KELVIN SHAWN SEALEY, 1997

Poverty is too expensive. We can't afford it any more.
QUINN BRISBEN, 1992

In the final analysis, the rich must not ignore the poor because both rich and poor are tied together. They entered the same mysterious gateway of human birth, into the same adventure of mortal life.

The agony of the poor impoverishes the rich; the betterment of the poor enriches the rich. We are inevitably our brother's keeper because we are our brother's brother. Whatever affects one directly affects all indirectly.

There is nothing new about poverty. What is new, however, is that we now have the resources to get rid of it.

A nation that continues year after year to spend more money on military defense than on programs of social uplift is approaching spiritual death.

MARTIN LUTHER KING, JR.
1967

The daily life of the Negro is still lived in the basement of the Great Society. He is still at the bottom despite the few who have penetrated to slightly higher levels. Even where the door has been forced partially open, mobility for the Negro is still sharply restricted. There is often no bottom at which to start, and when there is, there is almost always no room at the top.

All too many of those who live in affluent America ignore those who exist in poor America; in doing so, the affluent Americans will eventually have to face themselves with the question: How responsible am I for the well-being of my fellows? To ignore evil is to be an accomplice to it.

The contemporary tendency in our society is to base our distribution on scarcity, which has vanished, and to compress our abundance into the overfed mouths of the middle and upper classes until they gag with superfluity. If democracy is to have breadth of meaning, it is necessary to adjust this inequity.

From issues of personal dignity, [Negroes] are now advancing to programs that impinge upon the basic system of social and economic control. At this level Negro programs go beyond race and deal with economic inequality, wherever it exists.

There is nothing but a lack of social vision to prevent us from paying an adequate wage to every American citizen . . . There is nothing except shortsightedness to prevent us from guaranteeing an annual minimum — and *livable* — income for every American family.

MARTIN LUTHER KING, JR., 1967

The economic highway to power has few entry lanes for Negroes.
MARTIN LUTHER KING, JR., 1967

Equal opportunity

My fight is not *for* racial sameness but for racial equality and *against* racial prejudice and discrimination.
JOHN OLIVER KILLENS, 1964

Offering [the impoverished Negro] equal rights, even equal opportunity, at this late date without giving him a special boost is the kind of cruel joke American individualism has played on the poor throughout history.
JAMES FARMER, 1965

Unless we start to fight and defeat the enemies in our own country, poverty and racism, and make our talk of equality and opportunity ring true, we are exposed in the eyes of the world as hypocrites when we talk about making people free.
SHIRLEY CHISHOLM, 1970

I refuse to let my personal success, as part of a fraction of one per cent of the Negro people, explain away the injustices to fourteen million of my people . . . I fight for the right of the Negro people . . . to have decent homes, decent jobs, and the dignity that belongs to every human being.
PAUL ROBESON, 1949

[Jackie Robinson] was twenty years old as he hurtled through his first brilliant year at UCLA, but he was already old, old in the ways that James Baldwin would say any young black man was old growing up in America. He had already been marked so that he knew all too well where he was and was not going.
DAVID FALKNER, 1995

An increasing number of white Americans will assent to the proposition that Negroes should share more fully, even equally, in the good things of American life. At the same time an increasing number are demonstrating that they are unwilling to give up any part of their share of these good things.
LEWIS M. KILLIAN, 1968

America will not have racial equality until opportunities are equalized, beginning at the preschool level, to build up the supply of qualified applicants for the new jobs emerging in information-age America. The American ideal of equal opportunity still produces rewards, when it is given a real try. It needs to be tried more often.
CLARENCE PAGE, 1996

All we want is what you want, no less and no more.
SHIRLEY CHISHOLM, 1970

These people who now call for the end of policies to promote equal opportunity say there's been so much progress that no more such efforts are justified. But they fail to recognize that the tap root of racism is almost 400 years long.

VICE PRESIDENT AL GORE, 1998

Our Constitution and our national conscience demand that every American be accorded dignity and respect, receive the same treatment under the law, and enjoy equal opportunity.

COLIN POWELL, 1995

In the long run, there has to be something like equal opportunity for all kids to get a good education in this country. Better-off people will always have an advantage, but equal opportunity should be a goal, an aspiration.

ALBERT CARNESALE, 1997

[As Malcolm X said], if you've had a knife in my back for four hundred years, am I supposed to thank you for pulling it out? . . . The very least of your responsibility now is to compensate me, however inadequately, for centuries of degradation and disenfranchisement by granting peacefully — before I take them forcefully — the same rights and opportunities for a decent life that you've taken for granted as an American birthright.

ELDRIDGE CLEAVER, 1969

Debates over affirmative action, of qualifications versus quotas, deflect attention from more chronic disparities; in fact, that may be their purpose. At issue is whether government can or will commit itself to so raise black Americans that they will stand on a social and economic parity with members of other races.

What black Americans want is no more nor less than what white Americans want: a fair chance for steady employment at decent pay. But this opportunity has been one that the nation's economy continues to withhold. To be black in America is to know that you remain last in line . . . [and] have much less choice among jobs than workers who are white.

ANDREW HACKER, 1992

We must go beyond addressing the symptoms of poverty to treating the causes of poverty. Toward that end, the challenge is to evolve an economy that includes everybody and accords a fair chance to every American. . . . If this country's monumental problems are to be solved to everyone's betterment, the disenfranchised must be given a realistic opportunity to apply themselves to economic achievement.

ANDREW YOUNG, 1996

I'm not asking for any more or any less than anybody else. But just give me a chance to fail.

KEN GRIFFEY, SR., 1998

Affirmative action

Affirmative action originated in the 1960s to remedy and to prevent discrimination — primarily in employment and education — for all historically disadvantaged minorities and for women. It was later extended to Vietnam veterans and people with disabilities.

Contrary to what some critics say, affirmative action, when it works properly, guarantees only equal opportunity, not equal results.

Affirmative action is not a perfect remedy, but it beats the alternative, if the only alternative is to do nothing.
CLARENCE PAGE, 1996

The remedial justification for affirmative action asks about the extent of present discrimination, the risk of future discrimination, and the lingering effects from the past.
CHRISTOPHER EDLEY, JR., 1996

Defending affirmative action often feels like talking to someone who owns the remote control to all human discourse. The words explaining affirmative action, carefully chosen to cross great divides, disappear; mouths move, but no one listens.
CHARLES R. LAWRENCE III / MARI J. MATSUDA, 1997

This is a day which demands new thinking and the re-evaluation of old concepts. A society that has done something special *against* the Negro for hundreds of years must now do something special *for* him, in order to equip him to compete on a just and equal basis.
MARTIN LUTHER KING, JR., 1967

The issue of affirmative action is absolutely critical in America today. . . . When you see our country, and see how diverse it really is . . . you wonder, how are we going to be able to prevent a revolution in five or twenty or thirty years from now when all of these young people begin to realize they're not part of the social fabric, the economic fabric, the political fabric of America.
REPRESENTATIVE ROBERT MATSUI, 1998

Blacks were held back for two centuries of slavery plus another century of legally sanctioned subjugation and humiliation. One does not, as President Lyndon Johnson once said, hold some people back that long, then tell them they are free to run the race the same as everyone else.
CLARENCE PAGE, 1996

Tolerance and understanding won't "trickle down" in our society any more than wealth does.
MUHAMMAD ALI, 1996

Fairness as well as logic requires that special consideration be given to people who have been locked out of the economic mainstream.
ANDREW YOUNG, 1996

Except in very narrow court-ordered remedial circumstances of a last-resort nature, any affirmative action program must consider race flexibly, as one of several factors, and numerical goals must be true goals, rather than quotas.
CHRISTOPHER EDLEY, JR., 1996

The example of the Army is a good place to start a conversation about affirmative action. Long before it was fashionable, the Army was re-examining traditional standards.
LANI GUINIER, 1997

If there were social democratic redistributive measures that wiped out black poverty, and if racial and sexual discrimination could be abated through the good will and meritorious judgments of those in power, affirmative action would be unnecessary.
CORNEL WEST, 1993

If American society had the strength to do what should be done to ensure that justice prevails for all, then affirmative action would be exposed for what it is: an insult to the people it is intended to help. What I and others want is an equal chance, under one set of rules . . . While rules are different for different people, devices like affirmative action are needed to prevent explosions of anger.
ARTHUR ASHE, 1993

If a history of discrimination has made it difficult for certain Americans to meet standards, it is only fair to provide temporary means to help them catch up and compete on equal terms. Affirmative action in the best sense promotes equal consideration, not reverse discrimination.
COLIN POWELL, 1995

We would do well . . . to put the matter of courts, laws, and litigation to one side. We should focus instead on deciding what we believe to be right, for any given institution and set of circumstances.

When setting priorities, designers of affirmative action have to be very careful, but not compulsive. They should be concerned about criticism and litigation, but not obsessive about research or constipated by caution. Life must go on; the goal is justice, not perfection.
CHRISTOPHER EDLEY, JR., 1996

The . . . signs of racial apartheid are long gone, but news accounts of discrimination continue.
CLARENCE PAGE, 1996

Over the past thirty years, affirmative action has turned out to be one of the most controversial and divisive aspects of the debate on racism, framed in opposing perceptions of issues like "preferences," "quotas," "reverse discrimination," and "stigma."

I really believe that these debates turn more on how the initiative is described as opposed to what the problem is and whether we can reach agreement on how to solve it.

PRESIDENT BILL CLINTON
(December 17) 1997

The affirmative action debate, as it is largely presented, focuses on abstract ideas outside of social context — ideas like "colorblind" discussed without the history of racism; ideas like "preference" discussed outside the context of widening class division; ideas like "merit" discussed without reference to social structures like patriarchy.

CHARLES R. LAWRENCE III /
MARI J. MATSUDA, 1997

A number of whites dislike the idea . . . so much and perceive it to be so unfair that they have come to dislike blacks as a consequence. Hence the special irony of the contemporary politics of race. In the very effort to make things better, we have made some things worse. Strong arguments can be made in behalf of affirmative action, but its political price must also be recognized. Wishing to close the racial divide in America, we have widened it.

PAUL M. SNIDERMAN / THOMAS PIAZZA, 1993

We do not say that [preferences] make no difference whatsoever. We do say that they haven't made as much difference as is widely attributed to them and that they carry with them a very high cost. When it comes to race, the test of any public policy is, Will it bring us together or divide us? Preferences flunk that test.

ABIGAIL THERNSTROM, 1998

Talking about what we call preferences . . . is central to the discussion about race. Yes, there is a problem in America. . . . one that's complex, multidimensional. . . . But we can't get to the problem of moving this nation forward with respect to the issue of race unless we deal with the perception by a large number of people that there are preferences that are being given to people simply because they check a box.   WARD CONNERLY, 1997

Not all white Americans are biased . . . but all white Americans have been affected by bias.
LERONE BENNETT, JR., 1965

The most unusual aspects of this debate . . . are that only a minuscule number of Euro-Americans even claim to have been adversely affected by it, and the majority of Euro-American workers actually express support for it when it is explained in unbiased terms.
ORLANDO PATTERSON, 1997

You can look at [the] figures and ask, why are black folks making such a big deal out of affirmative action? That's the wrong question. The real question is why are white folks making such a big deal of it?
CHRISTOPHER EDLEY, JR., 1997

The rhetoric of reverse discrimination and racial preference erases the statistical reality of inordinate advantage and preference that come from being white and male in this country, creating a surreal landscape for public debate.
CHARLES R. LAWRENCE III / MARI J. MATSUDA, 1997

Given the fact that the average white household's net worth is *ten times* that of a black family's, and that the overwhelming majority of leaders in business, government, banking, and the media are upper-class white males, the argument that whites suffer "reverse discrimination" is absurd. Justice demands affirmative action based on race and gender to address continuing patterns of inequality in America. MANNING MARABLE, 1997

It would be disingenuous to deny that some white men — and perhaps even some white women — did not get jobs that . . . might otherwise have gone to them. Some of these individuals may be quite bitter about having been kept from positions they feel they worked for and deserved. So long as there are a limited number of desirable jobs . . . there are going to be disappointed people. . . . But given the disappointments that so often accompany having a black skin, it could be argued that whites should give way just a little. ANDREW HACKER, 1992

Opponents of effective affirmative action . . . argue that white rights are at stake and must not be compromised. This is a straightforward issue, and the position you take on it depends on which you care about more: the moral and worldly urgency of African-American progress or the moral and other consequences of deviating from the newly embraced principle of a color-blind society.

There are few howls about merit when it comes to college preferences for alumni or musicians or would-be social workers. Somehow "merit" can be stretched to encompass these preferences. Race is different, it seems. And . . . the question of *why* race is different is the very heart of the debate. CHRISTOPHER EDLEY, JR., 1996

As long as [affirmative action] was functioning the other way, there was . . . no opposition at all.
JOHN HOPE FRANKLIN, (January 12) 1998

Whites have always had . . . preferential treatment. Trying to level that playing ground sometimes is made to seem not working in the interest of all Americans because some people get disadvantaged as a result. . . . We do need to talk about how to do it fairly.   RONALD FOWLER, 1997

This whole business of affirmative action was no problem at all till the jobs run out. It's no big thing when you're on the job. If the lion and the deer is both full, nobody attacks. It's only when the lion gets hungry, he really fights for the thing.   FRANK LUMPKIN, 1992

The illusion of classlessness among whites led them to believe that all whites had opportunities to do this, that, and the other until the blacks came along. Every psychologist knows there are individual differences in every group. Every white applicant for say, a policemans's job, believing he'd get the job or promotion were it not for affirmative action, is engaging in a fascinating sort of idiocy.
KENNETH B. CLARK, 1992

How, it is asked, can people go through life, knowing that they have been hired not on their inherent talents, but to fill some quota or to satisfy appearances? Not surprisingly, white people seem to do most of the worrying about this apparent harm to black self-esteem. In fact, there is little evidence that those who have been aided by affirmative action feel many doubts or misgivings. For one thing, most of them believe they are entitled to whatever opportunities they have received. . . . Nor should it be forgotten that feelings of unworthiness seldom plague white Americans who have profited from more traditional forms of preferment.   ANDREW HACKER, 1992

Affirmative action in the 1990s shows how innocent and even victimized white Americans now feel compared to how insecure and embattled black people continue to feel.
CLARENCE PAGE, 1996

Despite the color-blind theory, white claims of reverse racism and preferential treatment for blacks, there is no queue of whites claiming black heritage to qualify for the "benefits" of black membership.
ROBERT STAPLES, 1993

To be concerned only with the white applicants who don't get the job, and not with the people of color who don't, is showing racial preference.
PAUL KIVEL, 1993

Whites move to the head of the line simply by being born White.
HARLON L. DALTON, 1995

My view . . . has always been that affirmative action has a cost; that part of the cost is the risk of stigma; but that the stigma I may suffer is a small price compared to the price I would pay if I faced closed doors, or . . . the price paid by crusaders a generation ago who faced vilification, mobs, beatings, and even murder.

CHRISTOPHER EDLEY, JR., 1996

Of all the arguments I have heard various people make against affirmative action, I find the least persuasive to be the charge that it makes its recipients feel bad. . . . When [Barbara Babcock] was asked in a press conference how it felt to think that she had gotten the job [in the Justice Department] because she was a woman, she replied that it felt a lot better than thinking she had *not* gotten the job because she was a woman. . . Most white males have not felt particularly bad about the special preferences they have received because of their race and gender for thousands of years.

CLARENCE PAGE, 1996

Mobility by means of affirmative action breeds tenuous self-respect and questionable peer acceptance for middle-class blacks. The new black conservatives voiced these feelings in the forms of attacks on affirmative action programs (despite the fact that they had achieved their positions by means of such programs).

CORNEL WEST, 1993

Many corporate executives have learned to live with affirmative action over the years, and even to welcome what they thought were clear rules that enabled them to increase diversity in their work forces without inviting lawsuits.

LINDA GREENHOUSE, 1997

Some people have claimed that affirmative action programs lower self-esteem in those who are favored by them . . . It seems to be something that white people worry about more than people of color.

PAUL KIVEL, 1993

Every corporate board, every university, every union, every branch of the media, should make full integration its goal and should accelerate affirmative action initiatives to achieve that goal today. There is no reason, given the wealth of talent available, to continue exclusion in these institutions.

CHARLES R. LAWRENCE III / MARI J. MATSUDA, 1997

The whole country can . . . agree that slavery is bad—and still come to blows over affirmative action.

FRANK RICH, 1997

Affirmative action has not been perfect in America — that's why two years ago we began an effort to fix the things that are wrong with it — but when used in the right way, it has worked. It has given us a whole generation of professionals in fields that used to be exclusive clubs — where people like me got the benefit of 100 percent affirmative action.

PRESIDENT BILL CLINTON, (June 14) 1997

The new black conservatives assume that without affirmative action programs, white Americans will make choices on merit rather than on race. Yet they have adduced no evidence for this. Most Americans realize that job-hiring choices are made both on reasons of merit and on personal grounds. And it is this personal dimension that is often influenced by racist perceptions.

CORNEL WEST, 1993

One of the reasons that it often makes sense to use affirmative action to lever open the doors is that they are closed for reasons other than a racist desire to oppress; they are closed, rather, because of the prevailing racialist stereotypes that render black people beneath the notice of white people. . . . . Once they take notice, quality will out.

STEPHEN L. CARTER, 1993

It is crucial that at this stage of backlash against the gains of the last three decades, we don't abandon one tool that we know works. . . . The hypocrisy is clear when white people who say they support equal opportunity attack affirmative action, yet want to leave intact the basic economic and racial injustices it is designed to correct.

PAUL KIVEL, 1993

What needs to be stressed is that despite all the controversies surrounding affirmative action, fewer blacks now have steady jobs of any kind and their unemployment rates have been growing progressively worse relative to those recorded for whites.

ANDREW HACKER, 1992

If we honestly add up the benefits of whiteness and the disadvantages of being a person of color, we can see that existing affirmative action programs don't go very far toward leveling the playing field.

PAUL KIVEL, 1993

Racism is an equal opportunity hazard.
CLYDE W. FORD, 1994

Mend, don't end, affirmative action, so that all Americans can have a fair chance at living the American dream.

PRESIDENT BILL CLINTON
(December 15) 1997

To that we add "and expand it." Reach out and pull up the many who wish to stand beside you — not above you, not below you — to bring their hands, too, to the task of rebuilding our land.

Nondiscrimination is not enough when powerful state-supported forces systematically keep some people out of the social world: devalued, silenced, casually violated. In a time when so many say affirmative action has gone too far, we say it has not gone far enough.

CHARLES R. LAWRENCE III /
MARI J. MATSUDA, 1997

We use affirmative action all the time. It is not by looking at academic merits alone that we have a football team with a 9-2 record, going to a bowl. . . . The fact is that, in California and everywhere, values apart from test scores do figure in university admissions policies — and should. A society that has prospered in diversity cannot want monochrome higher education.

ALBERT CARNESALE, 1997

For all its imperfections, affirmative action has made a major difference in the lives of women and minorities, in the process helping to realize, as no other policy has done, the nation's constitutional commitment to the ideals of equality, fairness, and economic integration. In utilitarian terms it is hard to find a program that has brought so much gain to so many at so little cost.

The continued institutional and direct discriminatory biases against Afro-Americans and women in the workplace require that affirmative action continue for at least another fifteen years. . . . After a quarter of a century, the time has come to think about not only how to extend it for a while longer, but how to phase it out with as much grace and as little harm as possible.

ORLÁNDO PATTERSON, 1997

When will affirmative action end in the United States? If we mean "end entirely and for all situations," the answer is simple: it should end when the justification for it no longer exists, when America has achieved racial justice in reality.

CHRISTOPHER EDLEY, JR., 1996

The genie of subtle racial intolerance is out of the bottle and not easily recaptured.

CHRISTOPHER EDLEY, JR., 1996

Color blindness . . .

All of us should embrace the vision of a colorblind society, but recognize the fact that we are not there yet and we cannot slam shut the doors of educational and economic opportunity.
PRESIDENT BILL CLINTON
(September 25) 1997

Total repression of attention to difference is not possible, not even desirable. So color blindness, as either goal or method, is far from being straightforward.

Why does color matter? When I hear this question, I often just sigh. Deeply. It's almost too basic a question to be answered. . . . But the need for an explanation is symptomatic of our divisions.
CHRISTOPHER EDLEY, JR., 1996

Neither the courts nor the Congress nor the president can declare . . . that the United States is a color-blind society. . . . Those who insist that we should conduct ourselves as if such a utopian state already existed have no interest in achieving it and, indeed, would be horrified if we even approached it. JOHN HOPE FRANKLIN, 1993

It is ironic that some of the modern apostles of apathy now misappropriate Dr. King's own words to support their belief that the struggle for justice in which he led us is nearly over . . . The phrase "the content of our character" takes on a different meaning when it is used by people who pretend that that is all we need to establish a color-blind society. They use their color blind the way duck hunters use a duck blind. They hide behind the phrase and just hope that we, like the ducks, can't see through it. VICE PRESIDENT AL GORE, 1998

The "color-blind theory" . . . has as its main premise that after 365 years of slavery and legal segregation, only 25 years of governmental laws and actions were necessary to reverse the historical systematic and legalized segregation and inequality in this country, and no further remedial effort is needed. The net effect of the color-blind theory is to institutionalize and stabilize the status quo of race relations for the twenty-first century: white privilege and black deprivation. . . . This does not sound like the racial utopia Martin Luther King dreamed of. Indeed, it may be his worst nightmare. ROBERT STAPLES, 1993

If we are blind to anything, it is not to color but to the effects of color in our society.
PROJECT HIP-HOP, 1997

The law should be "color-blind," the Supreme Court's conservative majority tells us. Yet our society is not. We Americans must deal with that sad fact or it will forever deal with us.

Perhaps the much-touted, widely cherished 1960s goal of a color-blind society is not possible. As long as we remain sighted, we remain inexorably color-conscious, and that is not totally bad.

The obligation to make America work as a "color-blind society," one in which all will be judged as Dr. King dreamed, by the content of our character and not by the color of our skin, is not up to its people of color alone. White people must also do their part.

CLARENCE PAGE, 1996

The evolution of the ideal color-blind society is imagined to occur more within feelings than in response to policy change; the ideal society's origins lie not in the resolution of complex group conflict but in mysterious, irreversible movements of the passionate heart.

BENJAMIN DEMOTT, 1995

The ideal of a color-blind society is a pale imitation of a greater, grander ideal: of living in a society where our color won't be denigrated, where our skin will be neither a badge for undue privilege nor a sign of social stigma. Because skin, race, and color have in the past been the basis for social inequality, they must play a role in righting the social wrongs on which our society has been built. We can't afford to be blind to color when extreme color consciousness continues to mold the fabric and form of our nation's history.

MICHAEL ERIC DYSON, 1996

Our thinking about the nation's most pressing social problems has become deeply "racialized"— saturated with attitudes, beliefs, and fears about race. We tend to dance around this fact whenever we publicly debate social policy. In our zeal to approach issues in a "color-blind" fashion, we often push their complex and volatile racial dimensions underground.

To not notice race is to miss one of the central ways in which power, position, and material well-being are distributed in our society. To not notice race is to be oblivious to the concerns of those below us in the pecking order and to lower our defenses against those above.

HARLON L. DALTON, 1995

A color-blind society does not exist in the United States and never has existed.

JOHN HOPE FRANKLIN, 1993

Instead of . . . nasty people intent on using our color against us, we are surrounded by perfectly nice people who embrace the color-blind ideal with a vengeance.
HARLON L. DALTON, 1995

To argue that we should begin to solve the problem of "racial" exclusion by assuming a color-blind world is to assume away the very problem we are trying to solve: only voodoo priests and rational choice theorists can get away with this kind of mumbo-jumbo.
ORLANDO PATTERSON, 1997

Since honest talk about our nation's racism is essentially off-limits, the old-time politics of race baiting has returned, disguised in the liberal rhetoric of colorblindness. . . . To believe that we live in a colorblind society, free of the legacy of slavery and segregation, is to deny what we see and hear every day.
CHARLES R. LAWRENCE III / MARI J. MATSUDA, 1997

It is disingenuous in the extreme to argue . . . that because the ideal of the civil rights movement, and of all persons of ethnic good will, is a color-blind world, any policy that takes account of African ancestry betrays this ideal.
ORLANDO PATTERSON, 1997

Too much has been made of the virtue of "color-blindness." I don't want Americans to be blind to my color as long as color continues to make a profound difference in determining life chances and opportunities. Nor do I wish to see so significant a part of my identity denied.

The "forgetting of race" . . . will not become a reality by rendering black life invisible . . . in a way that denies their humanity and tells them that their 350 years of history and life in America count for nothing. Inequality breeds distrust, resentment, and contempt. To sit down together at the great table of brotherhood in peace and comfort, we must do it as equal partners, not as dominant and submissive.
CLARENCE PAGE, 1996

"Color-blindness" is no virtue if it means denial of differences in the experience, culture, and psychology of black Americans and other Americans. These differences are not genetic, nor do they represent a hierarchy of "superior" and "inferior" qualities. But to ignore the formative influence of substantial differences in history and social existence is a monumental error.

The white psychiatrist who likes to think he is "color blind" may be as far off the mark as the psychiatrist who is blinded by color.
ALEXANDER THOMAS, M.D., 1972

America . . . has been best placed to prove the uselessness and obsolescence of the concept of color.
JAMES BALDWIN, 1963

The very notion of blindness about color constitutes an ideological confusion at best, and denial at its very worst.
PATRICIA WILLIAMS, 1997

On occasion, people move from trying to ignore race to explicitly pronouncing it irrelevant. A typical claim is: "I don't think of you as Black" . . . When I am on the receiving end of such a "compliment," I am tempted to respond, "Really? What *do* you think of me as?"
HARLON L. DALTON, 1995

While . . . I embrace color-blindness as a legitimate hope for the future, I worry that we tend to enshrine the notion with a kind of utopianism whose naïveté will ensure its elusiveness. In the material world ranging from playgrounds to politics, our ideals perhaps need more thoughtful, albeit more complicated, guardianship. By this I mean something more than . . . "I don't think about color, therefore your problems don't exist." If only it were so easy.
PATRICIA WILLIAMS, 1997

I, for one, am growing weary of those well-meaning white liberals who are forever telling me they don't know what color I am. The very fact that they single me out at the cocktail party and gratuitously make me the beneficiary of their blessed assurance gives the lie to their pronouncements.
JOHN OLIVER KILLENS, 1964

PROMOTING RACIAL UNDERSTANDING

It's just important that we're people rowing. They shouldn't see us as African-American rowers.
NOAH HICKS, 1997

. . . and our children

Children are the bearers of life in its simplest and most joyous form. Children are color-blind and still free of all the complications, greed, and hatred that will slowly be instilled in them through life.　　KEITH HARING, 1986

Color blindness comes naturally to children, who have not been taught the many ubiquitous lessons of racial life, values, and etiquette in America.
CLARENCE PAGE, 1996

In those first days in the South . . . a white kid of nine or ten was hanging over the roof of the Royals' dugout. Above the chorus of boos, [Jackie] Robinson could hear him shouting, "Atta boy, Jackie, nice try! Atta boy, Jackie!" . . . He knew that never in his life would he forget the face of this boy who was honest at heart, not yet filled with the poison of prejudice, who shouted a word of encouragement above the cries of the mob.
CARL T. ROWAN, 1960

White children in this country have no feeling about Negro children, other than the feelings all children have about each other, until it is taught to them.
MARGARET HALSEY, 1946

Surely few crimes are more tragic than the crime of fostering in children a false view of what man is by teaching them to believe that any other humans are basically different in their human needs or in their response to the frustration of those needs. This concept of fellow human beings as "other" is at the base of all racism.
JOHN HOWARD GRIFFIN, 1977

I wheel my two-year-old daughter in a shopping cart through a supermarket . . . and a little white girl riding past in her mother's cart calls out excitedly, "Oh look, Mommy, a baby maid!" And your mother shushes you, but she does not correct you.　　AUDRE LORDE, 1981

If they can just leave the young children alone, integration will do some good.
CHESTER DEVILLERS, 1991

You've got to be taught to hate and fear,
You've got to be taught from year to year,
It's got to be drummed in your dear little ear.
You've got to be carefully taught.

You've got to be taught to be afraid
Of people whose eyes are oddly made
And people whose skin is a diff'rent shade.
You've got to be carefully taught.

You've got to be taught before it's too late,
Before you are six or seven or eight,
To hate all the people your relatives hate.
You've got to be carefully taught.
You've got to be carefully taught.

OSCAR HAMMERSTEIN II, 1949

A young child . . . asks his mother why the man in the grocery store is so dark. Instead of answering, his mother tells him to be quiet, which tells the child it's not okay to discuss differences.

BEVERLY DANIEL TATUM
(May) 1998

Absence of prejudice is one of the virtues we ought to be trying to promote on a uniform basis throughout the country, and it ought to be part of the school curriculum.

PRESIDENT BILL CLINTON
(December 3) 1997

Our young must be taught that racial peculiarities do exist, but that beneath the skin, beyond the differing features and into the true heart of being, fundamentally, we are more alike, my friend, than we are unalike.

MAYA ANGELOU, 1993

BEST BUDDIES, 1990

© The Estate of Keith Haring

A key factor in preventing racism, say many psychologists, is to get children to talk about it.
ERIN BURNETTE, 1998

THE FUTURE

The faces and the tactics of the leaders
may change every four years, or two, or one,
but the people go on forever.
The people — beaten down today,
yet rising tomorrow;
losing the road one minute
but finding it the next;
their eyes always fixed on a star
of true brotherhood, equality and dignity
— *the people* are the real guardians
of our hopes and dreams.

PAUL ROBESON, 1952

ONE AMERICA: The President's Initiative on Race

Announcement by President Clinton
June 14, 1997

The greatest challenge we face . . . is also our greatest opportunity. . . . Can we fulfill the promise of America by embracing all our citizens of all races . . . can we become one America in the 21st century? . . . . Money cannot buy this goal, power cannot compel it, technology cannot create it. This is something that can come only from the human spirit.

If ten years from now people can look back and see that this year of honest dialogue and concerted action helped to lift the heavy burden of race from our children's future, we will have given a precious gift to America.

Town Meeting, Akron, Ohio
December 3, 1997

When you look to the future, you must . . . find a way to organize a continuing mechanism where people of good will can come together.

Our country has never really dealt with the race issue before except in an atmosphere of crisis and conflict and riots in the cities. So a lot of people . . . think I am nuts to be doing this. You know, what's the end, what's the point? The point is, making a more perfect union. The point is, proving we can have one America. The point is, it will be a lot more interesting, a lot more fun, and far more noble if we do it right.

I don't like it when people say we ought to tolerate our differences — I don't buy that. I think we ought to respect and celebrate our differences.

We're given a world that is much more interesting and exciting if we know and relate to people of different racial and other backgrounds. And it's up to us to decide what to do with it.

What we're trying to do here is drop a pebble in the pond and have it reverberate all across America.

Press Conference
December 17, 1997

I would like to . . . move beyond the I'm-for-it and you're-against-it stage to a more sophisticated and, ultimately, more meaningful debate. . . . What would you do to make sure that you didn't exclude whole groups who happen to be predominantly of racial minorities . . . predominantly poor, predominantly from difficult neighborhoods, predominantly born into families without the kinds of advantages many other children have. . . . And that debate is . . . in its infancy.

Talking and listening

In Congress, it's really interesting to hear these folks who don't want to do anything about it now criticize you for only wanting to talk about it. . . . Our answer has to be, you can't possibly do anything about race if you don't talk about it.

REPRESENTATIVE ELEANOR HOLMES NORTON, 1998

Racism is not easy to talk about in racially mixed company. It is often considered downright *impolite* to bring it up. Too many demons of guilt, resentment, and vulnerability are tied up in it. Unfortunately, it usually takes a racial eruption . . . to get Americans to acknowledge their racial differences in public and talk about them, at least for a while, before clamping the lid of denial back down.

CLARENCE PAGE, 1996

The problems of racism have not been solved and they will never be solved until we can learn to communicate with one another. Yet we have never listened to the words of minority spokesmen who have told us truths about ourselves and our country.

JOHN HOWARD GRIFFIN, 1977

We talk a lot and we talk pretty well about race, but we don't listen enough. And I'm hoping that if we listen to each other, we can begin to . . . make this society of ours into less and less of a country of strangers.

DAVID SHIPLER, 1997

It is time to "get real" about race and the persistence of racism in America.
DERRICK BELL, 1992

People are becoming more civil in the dialogue. That is a value that I think we need to cherish and deeply prize because in the celebration of our differences, we do need to be able to come together and say, you know, I kind of disagree, without saying you're racist because of that — so that persons can find the freedom to talk about the issues that deeply affect them.　　　RONALD FOWLER, 1997

We have utterly ignorant conversations about race in which my feelings are as valid as your feelings are as valid as her feelings, because nobody is dealing with any facts.　　　ROGER WILKINS, 1998

Conversation is critical, but not without self-reflection, both individually and communally. While myths help us make sense of the incomprehensible, they can also confine us, confuse us and leave us prey to historical laziness. Moreover, truth is not always easily discernible — and even when it is, the prism, depending on which side of the river you reside on, may create a wholly different illusion.　　　ALEX KOTLOWITZ, 1998

We have talked about racism over the years and talked about it and argued about it and fought about it and talked about it and wondered if, out of all those years, we learned a thing. I like to think that we have. Maybe it was something an audience member said. Maybe it's something you saw in the eyes of an interracial child that made you just think differently. Maybe those moments made you stop and think and, in a small way, open your heart a little wider.　　　OPRAH WINFREY, 1998

Having people feel free to disagree with people of different races without having somebody draw a racial inference, that's a huge thing. That's one of the benchmarks when you know you're getting where you need to be. (December 3)

I believe talking is better than fighting. And I believe when people don't talk and communicate and understand, their fears, their ignorance, and their problems are more likely to fester. (December 17)

Somewhere in here there's a way that we can get to . . . stop talking past each other and start working together. I cannot believe that 90 percent of the people in this country don't want the same kind of country in terms of racial matters. (December 19)
PRESIDENT BILL CLINTON, 1997

We need to talk with each other, honestly, simply, caringly.
PAUL KIVEL, 1993

By doing our homework we can transform a pretend conversation that seeks to simplify the impact of race in America into a full-scale dialogue that reveals the utter complexity, variability, and adaptability of racism.

Once the fig leaf has fallen, we might as well look at what it has been hiding. For it is by exploring the things we dare not say to each other that we can best get to know one another.

Unlike those who counsel smoothing over our differences and pushing our fears to the side, I am convinced that the only way to truly heal the past and prepare for a more just future is to (as we used to say) let it all hang out.

The very process of racial engagement puts us all on the same plane. When we are open and honest with each other; when we abandon our hiding places, take risks, and own up to our own self-interest, when we place on the table our assumptions, fears, trepidations, and secret desires, *by that very act* we are connecting with one another as equals.
                              HARLON L. DALTON, 1995

Meetings on racial justice often resemble nothing so much as a bazaar filled with peddlers offering the all-purpose answer. . . . The reality is that the problem has no single or simple solution. If there is one answer, it lies in recognizing how complex the issue has become and in not using that complexity as an excuse for inaction.
                              ELLIS COSE, 1997

Even when we admit to racially discriminatory practices, we rarely admit we are racist. This kind of massive denial is not possible without a strictly enforced taboo against speaking publicly about racism.
              CHARLES R. LAWRENCE III / MARI J. MATSUDA, 1997

Our truncated public discussions of race suppress the best of who and what we are as a people because they fail to confront the complexity of the issue in a candid and critical manner.
              CORNEL WEST, 1993

While cynical politicians peddle the poison of "reverse discrimination," no genuine interracial dialogue is possible.
              MANNING MARABLE, 1997

Everyone is so quick to choose sides, to refute the other's myths and to pass on their own.
ALEX KOTLOWITZ, 1998

Person to person

What I came to find out was that black people had those same fears white people had. They don't want to lose their services. They don't want to have bad schools. They don't want the same things that white people don't want.
JIM KISH, 1992

Going to this [private] school gave me an opportunity to really get to know a white person. When that happens, you abandon some of your prejudices and begin to see that fundamentally these people are just like you.
CHARLISE LYLES, 1992

Whatever white people do not know about Negroes reveals, precisely and inexorably, what they do not know about themselves.
JAMES BALDWIN, 1963

Even as the evil walls of legal segregation were tumbling down . . . it occurred to me that my reality might never be quite the same as that experienced by my white friends. . . . Separated by thick walls of prejudice, we would view each other through windows of stained-glass perceptions, colored by our personal experiences.
CLARENCE PAGE, 1996

You can't feel a sense of community with someone you don't know. The point is not that exposure makes us see that our similarities are more significant than our differences — that may not even be true in particular circumstances — but that it gives us a better understanding of our differences, which encourages acceptance or accommodation to them.
CHRISTOPHER EDLEY, JR., 1996

Men often hate each other because they fear each other; they fear each other because they do not know each other; they do not know each other because they cannot communicate; they cannot communicate because they are separated.
A. PHILIP RANDOLPH

I believe in my bones that the things that separate us make up one percent of who we are, that ninety-nine percent of our lives are similar. . . . We have given so much over the years to that one percent, complexion, it's a travesty. It think it's one of the great tragedies of our species.
CHARLES JOHNSON, 1992

We're on this merry-go-round just once. The least we can do is get to know the people we're riding with.
TASHA KNIGHT, 1992

I don't believe in the perfectibility of white people anymore. . . . God, how I loved America in 1950 . . . I thought then that prejudice was an individual thing that would die in heart after heart after the Constitution and the true humanity of black people were demonstrated to the people of our country.　　ROGER WILKINS, 1982

> Prejudice is the world's biggest coward in the face of fact. Proximity — if we can get enough of it — can solve these problems of racial prejudice and bigotry.
> BRANCH RICKEY

It's "them" they're afraid of. So if I come into their neighborhood to rent an apartment or buy a house, they still see "them." If people could accept us as individuals, we would get a hell of a lot farther.
JULIAN JEFFERSON, 1992

> The ability of Negroes and whites to work together, to understand each other, will not be found readymade; it must be created by the fact of contact.
> MARTIN LUTHER KING, JR.
> 1967

A lot of white people think, hey, you're black, you're a criminal. Most black people see a white person, hey, all white people are rich. I know that's not true. How can you make a suggestion like that if you don't know the person, white or black?　　KEVIN ROBINSON, 1992

Employment will offer, in the immediate future, more opportunities for favorable contact than housing, education, or any other area of activity. That this is so is an essentially negative comment about other realms of American society.　　THOMAS F. PETTIGREW, 1971

> If we could find ways of getting people to work on common projects . . . racial divisions seem to disappear and friendships occur.
> THOMAS H. KEAN, 1997

If we can find constructive ways for people to work together, learn together, talk together, be together, that's the best shot we've got to avoid some of the horrible problems we see in the rest of the world, to avoid some of the difficult problems we've had in our own history, and to make progress on the problems that we still have here today.　　PRESIDENT BILL CLINTON, (December 3) 1997

During the war, when we had to do it, we did it together. . . . Critical times, man forgets color.
FRANK LUMPKIN, 1992

The more contact we have with people of color and with images and information about them, the more we are motivated and equipped to challenge racism. . . . This awareness can guide our action and enrich our lives.

PAUL KIVEL, 1993

We hoped that given exposure to blacks each person would grow naturally to challenge the myths and prejudices of prior generations and mature at his or her own pace.

ANDREW YOUNG, 1996

The whole barrier exists because most people never come together and sit down at a table . . . join together, break bread together, and celebrate their differences and their likenesses.

OPRAH WINFREY, 1998

Unlike any other place, the workplace brings together people who pursue common objectives. . . . They go together through similar failure and successes. And that creates bonds that really go way beyond whatever racial tensions may exist in society at large.

SAMIR GIBARA, 1997

It is one thing to throw people from different worlds together in a classroom or an Army boot camp and yet another thing to make them feel a connection that produces a sense of community and mutual commitment. More is needed than proximity.   CHRISTOPHER EDLEY, JR., 1996

The key to taming fear and reducing uncertainty is for all of us to find ways to actually experience racial equality firsthand. Today, before we reach the Promised Land. . . . Now, more than ever, opportunities exist for White people to deal with Blacks (and other people of color) as true peers; to, in effect, try equality on for size.   HARLON L. DALTON, 1995

The best strategy in face-to-face relations between individuals from different ethnic groups is the good old Golden Rule — do unto others as you would wish them to do unto you. . . . Like democracy, the Golden Rule may not be perfect, but in a multiethnic society such as America, it is by far the best and safest strategy when dealing with fellow citizens, especially ones as traditionally American as Afro-Americans. All that it requires is a modicum of good faith and a willingness to negotiate one's way around the tricky social situations inevitably encountered in heterogeneous societies.

ORLANDO PATTERSON, 1997

When people are forced to interact to survive, their prejudices diminish.
MUHAMMAD ALI, 1996

Working for change

Only by a union of intelligence and sympathy across the color-line in this critical period of the Republic shall justice and right triumph.
W.E.B. DU BOIS, 1903

The initiative, and the future, rest with those whites and blacks who have liberated themselves from the master/slave syndrome.
ELDRIDGE CLEAVER, 1968

There are many persons ready to do what is right because in their hearts they know it is right. But they hesitate, waiting for the other fellow to make the first move — and he, in turn, waits for you. The minute a person whose word means a great deal dares to take the openhearted and courageous way, many others follow.
MARIAN ANDERSON, 1956

There was no one in the astronaut corps who looked anything like me. There were no women, no Blacks, no Asians, no Latinos. I could not reconcile the term "United States space program" with an endeavor that did not involve anyone except white males. . . . Thousands of fans wrote thanking me for Uhura's inspiration. . . . Things had to change.
NICHELLE NICHOLS, 1994

At some point, you have to face up to your place in American society. To find out what that place is, you have to determine how far you can walk out on the plank without feeling uncomfortable by yourself.
ARTHUR ASHE, 1981

It does no service to the cause of racial equality for white people to content themselves with judging themselves to be nonracist. Few people outside the Klan or skinhead movements own up to all-out racism these days. White people must take the extra step. They must become antiracist.
CLARENCE PAGE, 1996

The question . . . is no longer what to do, but whether there is still time in which to do it.
CHARLES E. SILBERMAN, 1964

Americans of good-will, the nice decent church people, the well-meaning liberals, the good-hearted souls who themselves wouldn't lynch anyone, must begin to realize that they have to be more than passively good-hearted, more than church-goingly Christian, and much more than word-of-mouth in their liberalism.

LANGSTON HUGHES, 1943

Each generation must decide whether to dig defensive trenches or build bridges, and each of us must choose whether to participate in that decision or just let others decide for us and for our children.
CHRISTOPHER EDLEY, JR., 1996

Any honest examination of the national life proves how far we are from the standard of human freedom with which we began. The recovery of this standard demands of everyone who loves this country a hard look at himself, for the greatest achievements must begin somewhere, and they always begin with the person. If we are not capable of this examination, we may yet become one of the most distinguished and monumental failures in the history of nations.

JAMES BALDWIN, 1961

The American Negro problem is a problem in the heart of the American. It is there that the interracial tension has its focus. It is there that the decisive struggle goes on.
GUNNAR MYRDAL, 1942

Sometimes change comes not in the first round, but at the second, third or fourth. Change starts with one person questioning, challenging, speaking up and doing something to make a difference. We can each make a difference . . . because each of us is already part of the community where racism exists and thrives.   PAUL KIVEL, 1993

The struggle itself is the point. To stand for a brighter vision of human possibility gives life meaning; it is a refusal to participate in the murder of one's own spirit.
CHARLES R. LAWRENCE III / MARI J. MATSUDA, 1997

While the legal, material, and even superficial requirements to eradicate racism are well known, its psychological and more deeply spiritual requirements have been persistently neglected — namely, the oneness of the human family. It is this principle of oneness that needs to be the driving force behind the struggle of uniting the races.

SARA HARRINGTON, 1998

We have to "walk the walk" not just "talk the talk."
PAUL KIVEL, 1993

While many of us regard ourselves as powerless, the fact is that all of us have some sphere of influence in which we can work for change, even if it is just in our own network of family and friends.

BEVERLY DANIEL TATUM, 1998

Except worry, there is very little that a single individual, working alone, can do about improving race relations in this country. . . . You cannot be a thousand people, but you can join a thousand people, and the whole will be greater than the sum of its parts.

The people who are unprejudiced, but who . . . feel it is so hopeless there is no use trying . . . probably do just as much damage to the emotional atmosphere in which we are facing the problem as the fanatical Negrophobes.

MARGARET HALSEY, 1946

You had to decide: Am I going to change the world, or am I going to change me? Or maybe change the world a little bit, just by changing me? If I can get ahead, doesn't that help my people?   SADIE DELANY, 1993

If the moderates of the white South fail to act now, history will have to record that the greatest tragedy of this period of social transition was not the strident clamor of the bad people, but the appalling silence of the good people.

No social advance rolls in on the wheels of inevitability. Every step toward the goal of justice requires sacrifice, suffering, and struggle; the tireless exertions and passionate concern of dedicated individuals.

MARTIN LUTHER KING, JR., 1958

None of us alone can save the nation or world. But each of us can make a positive difference if we commit ourselves to do so.
CORNEL WEST, 1994

The tolerance and understanding necessary to heal must come from each and every one of us, arising out of our everyday conduct, until decency reaches a flood tide.
MUHAMMAD ALI, 1996

A wet blanket can never be the banner of freedom.
PAUL ROBESON, 1958

As an African-American man who attended school in the South, I could either shut my eyes to what's going on, or help to dismantle the problem. It is for my well-being to be part of something rather than dying a bit each day.   JOHN TUCKER, 1997

Voices within our community call us to turn inward, away from potential allies with whom we can work to achieve positive change. What is required is the definition of a new moral assignment, a new vision of human emancipation.   MANNING MARABLE, 1997

The solution to racism lies in our ability to see its ubiquity but not to concede its inevitability. It lies in the collective and institutional power to make change, at least as much as with the individual will to change. It also lies in the absolute moral imperative to break the childish, deadly circularity of centuries of blindness to the shimmering brilliance of our common, ordinary humanity.
                                        PATRICIA WILLIAMS, 1997

A nice lady in the back . . . asked what I thought about how we begin to move forward. I think it is up to each individual, which then moves to your family, which moves to your community. Each person, in their own life, let your life be a light for peace, for justice, for all that is good. Just let it shine, let it shine, let it shine, let it shine.
                                        OPRAH WINFREY, 1998

One of the less dismaying aspects of race relations in the United States is that their improvement is not a matter of a few people having a great deal of courage. It is a matter of a great many people having just a little courage.
                                        MARGARET HALSEY, 1946

By changing ourselves, we are doing the only thing we can do to change the world. To say that it is not enough is a lack of will, a lack of faith. It must be enough, for it is everything.
                                        SARA BULLARD, 1996

Power comes from coalitions, not through isolation or alienation from others.
                                        MANNING MARABLE, 1997

Keeping the dream alive

Through all the sorrow of the Sorrow Songs there breathes a hope — a faith in the ultimate justice of things. . . . Sometimes it is faith in life, sometimes a faith in death, sometimes assurance of boundless justice in some fair world beyond. But . . . the meaning is always clear: that sometime, somewhere, men will judge men by their souls and not by their skins.

Work, culture, liberty — all these we need, not singly but together, not successively but together, each growing and aiding each, and all striving toward that vaster ideal that swims before the Negro people, the ideal of human brotherhood.
W.E.B. DU BOIS, 1903

Let us all hope that the dark clouds of racial prejudice will soon pass away and the deep fog of misunderstanding will be lifted from our fear-drenched communities and in some not too distant tomorrow the radiant stars of love and brotherhood will shine over our great nation with all of their scintillating beauty.
MARTIN LUTHER KING, JR., (Letter) 1963

What is required now is an act of the spirit. We must abandon our shallow trenches and confront each other as coinheritors of a common land, which is to say that we must meet and know each other as brothers in the marriage of visions, as coconspirators in the making of a dream, as fellow passengers on a journey into the unknown.
LERONE BENNETT, JR., 1964

America is free to choose whether the Negro shall remain her liability or become her opportunity.
GUNNAR MYRDAL, 1942

If we . . . the relatively conscious whites and the relatively conscious blacks . . . do not falter in our duty now, we may be able, handful that we are, to end the racial nightmare, and achieve our country, and change the history of the world. If we do not now dare everything, the fulfillment of that prophecy, re-created from the Bible in song by a slave, is upon us: *God gave Noah the rainbow sign, No more water, the fire next time!*

JAMES BALDWIN, 1963

I think white America has to be jolted into reality: if we do not devote the resources necessary to avert the tragedy, we will become a police state. . . . Will there have to be some sort of explosion, some sort of civil disorder, before we realize the gravity of the situation? Think of the money we instantly manufactured for Desert Storm. The crisis in this country is much more grave than that. But we don't have the same kind of will to tackle it. We have to. We simply have no choice.

SALIM MUWAKKIL, 1992

Comparing the reality here with the reality of societies in extremis is too easy. . . . It is fairer, and certainly right, instead, to compare American practice with America's ideals, and American life with America's dreams.

The continuing controversy . . . is about values and vision. What does America want to see in the mirror? What kind of communities do we want for our children? What dreams will nourish the spirits of the least among us? We have a history of division, but for the most part it is division based on our perspectives, not our dreams.

CHRISTOPHER EDLEY, JR., 1996

Let us hope and pray that the vast intelligence, imagination, humor, and courage of Americans will not fail us. Either we learn a new language of empathy and compassion, or the fire this time will consume us all.

CORNEL WEST, 1993

The task that remains is to cope with our interdependence — to see ourselves reflected in every other human being and to respect and honor our differences.

MELBA PATILLO BEALS, 1994

The socalled "racial problem" . . . requires . . . a new grasp of the meaning of the human experience.
LILLIAN SMITH, 1949

We know what the problem is; it has been well outlined statistically and historically. The problem is white racism. The problem is discrimination. The problem is racial prejudice. Now, what is the answer to the problems of black people? The answer is the will and power of white society and white institutions to change. They *must* change.

CHARLES H. KING, JR., 1983

Desegregation will break down the legal barriers and bring men together physically, but something must touch the hearts and souls of men so that they will come together spiritually because it is natural and right.

MARTIN LUTHER KING, JR.
1967

That perennial traveler — the visitor from Mars — would wonder how a democracy can harbor group prejudice, and why we are concerned with controlling and not with eliminating it. . . . Prejudice is not innate but acquired; is not congenital but parental; is a virus infection, not a vital function. One generation, he would say, was sufficient to eradicate smallpox, diphtheria, and other plagues. A much shorter period should suffice to inoculate against the plague of prejudice.

ABRAHAM RUBIN / GEORGE J. SEGAL, 1946

What we need is a new political vision that continues to take race seriously even as we search for new ways to transform its significance.

HARLON L. DALTON, 1995

Can we African Americans . . . prevent our outrage at the wrongs we have suffered in America from destroying our spirit, from depriving us of the high moral ground we once held? Can we avoid the temptation to sink utterly into despair, cynicism, and violence, and thus become abject prisoners of our past?

I see nothing inconsistent between being proud of oneself and one's ancestors and, at the same time, seeing oneself as first and foremost a member of the commonwealth of humanity, the commonwealth of all races and creeds. . . . I would ask that all Americans could see themselves that way, past the barbed-wire fences of race and color. We are the weaker for these divisions, and the stronger when we transcend them. ARTHUR ASHE, 1993

The failures of the past must not be an excuse for the inaction of the present and the future.
MARTIN LUTHER KING, JR., 1967

Nothing venture, nothing gain. If you embark on a project as magnificent in concept as the brotherhood of man, it is foolish not to anticipate difficulties of proportionate magnificence.

The feelings, myths and prejudices about the Negro American which now seem so vivid and real to some of our white contemporaries will take their place on the shelf along with the belief in witches and the notion that the earth is the center of the solar system.

Nobody knows as yet whether the future [of the race situation] is hopeless. All we know is that it can be made hopeless, if enough people choose to consider it so.

MARGARET HALSEY, 1946

One of the biggest challenges that remains is to be able to weave people of all different colors and creeds into the beautiful tapestry of American life. . . . Eradicating racial differences can only happen when a generation of Americans becomes firmly convinced that race truly doesn't matter.

ARMSTRONG WILLIAMS, 1997

Although racism is still a central constituent of American life, we have made progress, things have changed . . . because the human spirit is indomitable and we each share that spirit. We can only sustain our efforts by building on and celebrating the achievements of the vast numbers of people who have contributed to getting us as far as we are today.

PAUL KIVEL, 1993

I can't say for sure what a racially just America would look like, but . . . we might discover that we are more united in what we desire for the future than in how we deal with the present. If so, we ought to consider working backward. By spending a little time dreaming together about the promised land, we just might figure out how to bring it about.

HARLON L. DALTON, 1995

All of the evidence suggests that most ordinary Americans have proven themselves extraordinary in their willingness to suffer the pain of ethnic change. . . . They do so because the truth has finally dawned on all but the most ethnically myopic that Afro-Americans are among the most American of Americans. . . because it is the right thing to do. . . because they know that integration, however difficult the journey, is the only way to go, and . . . because, as a nation, there can be no turning back.

ORLANDO PATTERSON, 1997

It's time for us as a country to try to come together in ways that freedom was really meant to be.

OPRAH WINFREY, 1998

We are a people determined to make it, not in spite of our blackness, but because of it. Historians will record it, social scientists will be astounded by it, and civilizations will be magnified by it.
CHARLES H. KING, JR., 1983

Our earth is but a small star in the great universe. Yet of it we can make, if we choose, a planet unvexed by war, untroubled by hunger or fear, undivided by senseless distinctions of race, color or theory.
STEPHEN VINCENT BENÉT, 1942

Are we — the nation that first embarked on the high adventure of making a world fit for human beings to live in — about to destroy ourselves because we have killed our dream? Can we live with a dead dream inside us? How many dead dreams will it take to destroy us all?
LILLIAN SMITH, 1961

The struggle to eliminate racism, war, and poverty is a burden, but in America, with all the freedom and opportunity afforded us under our Constitution, in the most productive society in human history, it is an easy burden if we undertake it together.   ANDREW YOUNG, 1996

America may not be the best nation on earth, but it has conceived loftier ideals and dreamed higher dreams than any other nation. America is a heterogeneous nation of many different people of different races, religions, and creeds. Should this experiment go forth and prosper, we will have offered humans a new way to look at life; should it fail, we will simply go the way of all failed civilizations.
NIKKI GIOVANNI, 1993

I do believe that wherever Gene [Roddenberry] may be, he will one day see his dream of the future unfold, not on a soundstage but in space, in a time when humankind's propensity for hatred and intolerance will be a memory.
NICHELLE NICHOLS, 1994

Evil must be attacked by . . . the day-to-day assault of the battering rams of justice.
MARTIN LUTHER KING, JR., 1967

Index / Sources

PLEASE NOTE: The dates in this list match those at the ends of the quotes.
Where more than one source is shown for an individual, use the date as a guide. [N.d. = no date in source.]

The VOICES: About the people who are quoted

PLEASE NOTE: Individuals are identified as of the time they wrote or spoke the quoted material.

Abdul-Jabbar, Kareem, formerly Lew Alcindor, UCLA honor student, basketball star

Ali, Muhammad, formerly Cassius Clay, champion boxer, world peace activist

Allport, Gordon, psychology professor, Harvard U.

Alter, Jonathan, senior editor and columnist, *Newsweek*

Anderson, Marian, renowned contralto, first black to sing at Metropolitan Opera [1897-1993]

Anderson, Michael, editor at *The New York Times Book Review*

Angelou, Maya, dancer, actress, poet

Asante, Molefi Kete, Professor and Chairperson, Department of African American Studies, Temple U., Philadelphia, Pennsylvania

Ashe, Arthur, tennis champion and activist, died of transfusion-related AIDS [1943-1993]

Axelrod, Alan, writer, editor, public historian

Baldwin, James, award-winning author of fiction and non-fiction [1924-1987]

Ball, Edward, author, *Slaves in the Family*

Bancroft, Hubert Howe, New England historian

Beals, Melba Patillo, communications consultant

Beatty, D. J., student, U. of Akron

Belafonte, Harry, singer, social activist

Bell, Derrick, Visiting Professor, New York U. Law School

Benét, Stephen Vincent, poet, author of *John Brown's Body*, Pulitzer Prize-winning narrative poem [1898-1943]

Bennett, Lerone, Jr., social historian, managing editor, *Ebony Magazine*

Bierce, Ambrose, author, journalist, satirist, disappeared in Mexico [1842-ca.1914]

Bloom, Julius (no information available)

Bloustein, Edward J., president, Rutgers U.

Bond, Julian, civil rights activist, history professor at U. of Virginia and American U., Chairman, NAACP National Board of Directors

Boyle, Sarah Patton, Virginian, activist for integration

Brisben, Quinn, retired high-school teacher

Brown, Ivor, London theater critic

Brown, Lloyd L., journalist, editor, author, close friend and associate of Paul Robeson

Bruce, Henry Clay, former slave

Bullard, Sara, editor, *Teaching Tolerance*, Southern Poverty Law Center

Burnette, Erin, staff reporter, *APA Monitor*

Burnham, Margaret, civil rights attorney, former judge

Campbell, Will D., self-styled "bootleg preacher," graduate of Yale Divinity School

Capraro, Jim, executive director, Greater Southwest Development Corporation, Chicago

Carmichael, Stokeley, Trinidad born, Harvard graduate, founding member Student Nonviolent Coordinating Committee, later Kwame Ture [1941-1998]

Carnesale, Albert, Chancellor, U. of California, Los Angeles

Carter, Stephen L., William Nelson Cromwell Professor of Law at Yale U.

Cartwright, Samuel, physician

Chavez-Thompson, Linda, executive vice-president A.F.L.-C.I.O., member President Clinton's Initiative on Race and Reconciliation

Chisholm, Shirley, first black Congresswoman, served seven terms, from 1968 to 1982

Clark, Kenneth B., psychologist and social scientist, director, Social Dynamics Research Institute, City College of New York

Cleaver, Eldridge, reformed criminal, Black Panther leader, radical activist [1935-1998]

Clinton, Bill [William Jefferson], President of the United States

Clinton, Hillary Rodham, First Lady of the United States

Coleman, Wanda, poet and novelist

Connerly, Ward, member, Board of Regents, U. of California

Cose, Ellis, contributing editor, *Newsweek*

Cowley, W. H., president, Hamilton College

Crockett, George W., Congressman from Michigan

Cuney-Hare, Maud, writer, musicologist [1874-1936]

Cuomo, Andrew, Secretary of Housing and Urban Development

Dalton, Harlon L., Professor, Yale Law School

Davis, Ossie, actor, playwright, activist, married to actor/activist Ruby Dee

Davis, Sammy, Jr., all-around entertainer [1925-1990]

Delany, Bessie, second black woman dentist in New York [1891-1995]

Delany, Sadie, first black to teach domestic science in New York high schools [1889-1999]

Delphin, Renee, Yale undergraduate

DeMott, Benjamin, writer, teacher, cultural critic

Devillers, Chester, retired mayor pro tem, Darien, McIntosh County, Georgia

Douglas, James, music critic, London Daily Express

Douglass, Frederick, escaped slave and self-taught reader and orator, powerful force in abolitionist movement [1817-1895]

Du Bois, W.E.B., Harvard graduate, writer, activist, professor of sociology, economics and history, a founder of NAACP (National Association for the Advancement of Colored People) and editor of *Crisis* [1868-1963]

Dunford, Judith, freelance writer, reviewer

Dyson, Michael Eric, professor, Communication Studies, U. of North Carolina, Chapel Hill

Early, Gerald, author, Director, Department of African-American Studies, Washington U.

Edelman, Rob, writer on film and baseball

Edley, Christopher, Jr., Professor, Harvard Law School

Edwards, Audrey, editor, *Essence* magazine

Eliot, T. S., poet, critic, playwright, 1948 Nobel Prize for Literature [1888-1965]

Falkner, David, author, *The Last Yankee*

Farmer, James, civil rights activist, founder of CORE (Congress of Racial Equality)

Fitzhugh, George, Virginia lawyer, writer and lecturer in defense of slavery [1804-1881]

Flood, Curt, All-Star baseball player, broke trading system, [1938-1997]

Foner, Philip S., teacher, historian, author and editor of numerous books on American, African-American, women's, and labor history [1910-1994]

Ford, Clyde W., press secretary and executive board member, Northern Puget Sound branch, NAACP

Forman, James, former Executive Secretary, Student Nonviolent Coordinating Committee (SNCC), former Minister of Education, Black Panther Party

Fowler, Pastor Ronald, minister in Akron, Ohio

Franklin, John Hope, James B. Duke Professor Emeritus of History and former Professor of Legal History, Law School at Duke U., chairman, President Clinton's Initiative on Race and Reconciliation

Freeman, Carol, executive secretary to chancellor, City College of Chicago

Gates, Henry Louis, Jr., W.E.B. Du Bois Professor of the Humanities and chairman, Afro-American Studies Department, Harvard U.

Gibara, Samir, Chairman and Chief Executive Officer, Goodyear Tire and Rubber Company

Gibson, Althea, first black tennis champion at U.S. Open and Wimbledon

Gilman, Sander L., Professor of German Literature, Cornell U., Professor of Psychiatry, Cornell Medical College

Giovanni, Nikki, poet, professor of English, Virginia Technical College

Glasser, Ira, executive director, American Civil Liberties Union

Gore, Al, Vice President of the United States

Graham, Lawrence Otis, president, Progressive Management Associates, White Plains, N.Y.

Greene, Melissa Faye, Atlanta journalist, author, *The Temple Bombing*

Greenhouse, Linda, reporter, *New York Times*

Griffey, Ken Sr., long-time major league baseball player, seeking managerial position

Griffin, John Howard, student of literature, medicine, music, philosophy, and intercultural communication, author of *Black Like Me*, and many other works of fiction and non-fiction

Guinier, Lani, law professor, U. of Pennsylvania

Gutierrez, Joe, union representative, former steel worker

Hacker, Andrew, professor of political science at Queens College, New York City

Halsey, Margaret, best-selling humorous author in the 1930s (*With Malice Toward Some*), became concerned about black/white relations when working in canteen for servicemen during World War II

Hamilton, Charles V., expert on civil rights and constitutional law, writer and activist

Hammerstein, Oscar, II, librettist and lyricist [1895-1960]

Hammond, James Henry, South Carolina lawyer, manager of ten-thousand-acre plantation and 147 slaves, later Congressman, Governor, Senator [1807-1864]

Haring, Keith, internationally popular, prolific artist, died of AIDS [1958-1990]

Harper, William, South Carolina lawyer, legislator, chancellor, judge, powerful advocate for states' rights [1790-1847]

Harrington, Sara, chairperson, Lexington [Mass.] Coalition for Racial Equality

Harris, Gloria, United Parcel Service striker

Herbert, Anita, criminal investigator for the IRS

Herbert, Bob, op ed columnist, *New York Times*

Hicks, Noah, 11-year-old brother of coxswain for Mandela, losing team in Boston's elite Head of the Charles Regatta

HIP-HOP, Project, ACLU of Mass., Nancy Murray, Director. High school students tour South, visiting key sites and meeting veterans of civil rights movement, then report on their experiences to students at local schools. (For information, call 617-482-3170.)

Hohri, Bill, computer programmer, first generation Japanese-American

Huckabee, Mike, Governor of Arkansas

Hughes, Langston, poet, playwright, novelist, columnist, activist [1902-1967]

Isaacs, Harold R., senior research associate, Center for International Studies at Massachusetts Institute of Technology

Jackson, Reverend Jesse, long-time civil rights leader

Jefferson, Julian, Chicago resident

Jefferson, Margo, Pulitzer Prize-winning cultural critic, book reviewer and theater critic, *The New York Times*

John Paul II, Pope since 1978

Johnson, Charles, teacher of American literature at U. of Washington, author, *Middle Passage*

Johnson, James Weldon, writer, civil rights leader, lawyer, diplomat, founded first black U.S. newspaper, lyricist, "Lift Every Voice and Sing" [1871-1938]

Jones, LeRoi, poet, playwright, social essayist (now Amiri Baraka)

Kean, Thomas H., former Governor of New Jersey, president of Drew U.

Kelly, Dawn, junior, U. of Illinois, Chicago, student government president, member, board of trustees

Killens, John Oliver, novelist, lecturer, writer for television and motion pictures

Killian, Lewis M., professor of sociology, Florida State U.

King, Reverend Bernice Albertine, a daughter of Martin Luther King, Jr.

King, Charles H., Jr., president, Urban Crisis Center, Atlanta, Georgia [deceased]

King, Coretta Scott, singer, founding president of the Martin Luther King, Jr., Center for Nonviolent Social Change, Atlanta, Georgia

King, Reverend Martin Luther, Jr., scholar, theologian, charismatic civil rights organizer, 1964 recipient of Nobel Peace Prize, assassinated [1929-1968]

Kish, Jim, manager of a shop

Kivel, Paul, nonviolence activist, co-founder Oakland [Cal.] Men's Project

Knight, Tasha, writer of software documentation

Kotlowitz, Alex, author, *The Other Side of the River: A Story of Two Towns, a Death and America's Dilemma*

Kranz, Rachel, author of books for young children

Langford, Keili, Yale University undergraduate

Latouche, John, poet, lyricist, librettist [deceased]

Lattimore, Joseph, insurance broker

Lawrence, Charles R., III, law professor, Georgetown U., married to Mari J. Matsuda, co-author, *Words That Wound*

Lee, Bill Lann, son of Chinese immigrants, civil liberties lawyer, appointed Acting Assistant Attorney General for Civil Rights and Counselor to the Attorney General for Civil Rights Enforcement

Lewis, John, National Chairman, Student Non-Violent Coordinating Committee

Lipsyte, Robert, sports columnist, *New York Times*

Lorde, Audre, poet, essayist, librarian, professor of creative writing [1934-1992]

Loury, Glenn C., director, Institute on Race and Social Division at Boston University

Lumpkin, Frank, retired steel worker

Lyles, Charlise, columnist, *Norfolk Pilot*, Virginia

Malcolm X, born Malcolm Little, former prisoner, convert to Nation of Islam, assassinated after breaking with Elijah Mohammad [1925-1965]

Maltin, Sam, sportswriter

Mann, Jean Tucker, Director of Social Work Services for U. of Maryland Medical System

Marable, Manning, Director, Institute for Research in African-American Studies, Columbia U.

Massery, Hazel Bryan, protester at Central High School integration taunted

Massey, Douglas, Professor of Sociology, U. of Chicago

Matsuda, Mari J., law professor, Georgetown U., married to Charles R. Lawrence III, co-author, *Words That Wound*

Matsui, Robert T., Democratic Congressman from California

McIntosh, Peggy, Associate Director, Wellesley College Center for Research on Women

McNair, Ronald, physicist, astronaut, killed in Shuttle Challenger explosion [1950-1986]

Mobley, Mamie, teacher, mother of Emmett Till, 14-year-old murdered in Mississippi (see p. 161)

Morehouse, Ward, regent, U. of California

Morganthau, Tom, letters correspondent, *Newsweek*

Morrison, Toni, teacher, editor, author of *The Bluest Eye, Sula, Song of Solomon, Beloved, Paradise*

Muwakkil, Salim, staff journalist, *In These Times*, alternative Chicago newspaper

Myrdal, Gunnar, Swedish lawyer, social scientist, asked to head study of race in America for Carnegie Corporation from 1938 to 1942

Nichols, Nichelle, singer, dancer, actress, activist, first African-American woman to have a major continuing role on television as Lieutenant Uhura of the Starship Enterprise in *Star Trek®*

Norton, Eleanor Holmes, Congresswoman representing District of Columbia

Nott, Josiah C., South Carolina surgeon, lecturer on anatomy, most prominent exponent of ethnology, the study of race differences [1804-1873]

Owen, Chandler, co-editor with A. Philip Randolph, *The Messenger*, "The Only Radical Negro Magazine in America"

Page, Clarence, columnist, *The Chicago Tribune*

Painter, Nell Irvin, author, *Sojourner Truth, A Life, A Symbol*, teacher at Princeton

Patterson, Orlando, historical sociologist, author and essayist, John Cowles Professor, Harvard U.

Pettigrew, Thomas F., Professor of Social Psychology, Harvard U.

Phillips, Charles, writer, editor, public historian

Piazza, Thomas, Research Specialist and Manager of Technical Services, U. of California, Berkeley

Polite, Craig K., psychologist

Powell, Colin L., former Chairman of the Joint Chiefs of Staff

Project HIP-HOP, *see* HIP-HOP

Rambler, Mark, editorial assistant, *Newsweek*

Randolph, A. Philip, organizer of Brotherhood of Sleeping Car Porters, civil rights activist, publisher, vice president AFL-CIO [1889-1979]

Rich, Frank, Op Ed columnist, *New York Times*

Rickey, Branch, president and general manager, Brooklyn Dodgers, recruited Jackie Robinson in 1947, breaking color line in major league baseball [1881-1965]

Ricks, Christopher, Professor of English, Boston U.

Robeson, Paul, internationally renowned singer, actor, activist [1898-1976]

Robinson, Jackie, all-around athlete and premature civil rights activist, broke color line in major league baseball but had to pledge not to react by word or action to any provocation [1919-1972]

Robinson, Joseph, president, Chicago local, United Steel Workers of America

Robinson, Kevin, criminal law major at a city college

Robinson, Maxie Cleveland, Sr., high-school history teacher and basketball coach, father of Randall Robinson

Robinson, Rachel, wife of Jackie, shared anguish of discrimination when they traveled in the South

Robinson, Randall, founder and president, Trans Africa, formed to influence U.S. policies toward Africa and the Caribbean

Roediger, David, chairman of American Studies, U. of Minnesota

Rogers, J. A., historian [1880-1966]

Rose, Arnold, social scientist, editor

Rowan, Carl T., foreign correspondent, diplomat, syndicated columnist for Chicago *Daily News*

Rubin, Abraham, vice president, National Smelting Co., Cleveland, Ohio, member, Board of the American Council on Race Relations

Russwurm, John B., co-founder, first black newspaper in the U.S. [1799-1851]

Sealey, Kelvin Shawn, founder, non-profit grant-making Obsidian Society

Segal, George J., assistant to Abraham Rubin, active in antidiscrimination fields

Sergeant, Elizabeth Shepley, writer for *The New Republic, Harper's Magazine*, and other contemporary journals [1881-1965]

Shipler, David K., former New York Times reporter, author, *A Country of Strangers: Black and White in America*

Silberman, Charles E., economist, member of Board of Editors, *Fortune* Magazine

Smith, Lillian, Southern white writer, educator, activist [1897-1966]

Sniderman, Paul M., Professor of Political Science, Stanford U.

Staples, Robert, Professor of Sociology, U. of California at San Francisco

Stevens, Hope R., attorney, noted Harlem civic and business leader, long-time friend of Paul Robeson

Stevenson, Norma, accountant, Chicago radio station

Swaffer, Hannen, British theater critic, gossip columnist

Tatum, Beverly Daniel, psychologist, professor at Mount Holyoke college, author, *Why Are the Black Kids Eating Together in the Cafeteria?*

Terkel, Studs, graduate of Chicago Law School, actor, sports commentator, disk jockey, talk-show host, Pulitzer Prize-winning author

Terry, Peggy, Chicago resident

Thernstrom, Abigail, senior fellow, Manhattan Institute, member, Massachusetts Board of Education

Thomas, Alexander, M.D., Professor of Psychiatry, New York U. Medical Center, and Director, Psychiatric Division, Bellevue Hospital

Thurman, Little Dovie, evangelist

Tucker, John, director, Racial Justice and Equity Project, Burlington, Vermont

Van Evrie, John H., Washington, D.C., physician and New York City publisher

Vivian, Reverend C. T., civil rights activist

von Hoffman, Constantine, freelance writer

Walton, Anthony, poet and esssayist

Washington, Booker T., former slave, founder of Tuskegee Institute, focused on teaching vocational skills [1856-1915]

Washington, William, father of tennis family

Wattleton, Faye, nurse, former president (first African-American) of Planned Parenthood

Werner, Fred, editor, student newspaper, U. of Illinois, Chicago

West, Cornel, Professor of Afro-American Studies and Philosophy of Religion, Harvard U.

Wicker, Tom, retired political columnist, *New York Times*

Wilkins, Roger, Pulitzer Prize-winning journalist, civil rights activist, former Assistant Attorney General of the United States

Williams, Armstrong, syndicated broadcast commentator and Los Angeles Times columnist

Williams, Patricia, professor of law, Columbia U., columnist, *The Nation* magazine

Williams, Robert F., expelled from NAACP for advocating armed militancy, self-exiled to Cuba and China

Winfrey, Oprah, actress, influential talk show host

Winter, William F., former Democratic Governor of Mississippi, member President Clinton's Initiative on Race and Reconciliation

Wolfe, Alan, University Professor, Boston U., sociologist

Wollstonecraft, Mary, pioneer British feminist writer, mother of Mary Shelley (author of *Frankenstein*) [1759-1797]

Woollcott, Alexander, essayist, raconteur, radio personality

Young, Andrew, minister, former executive director SCLC (Southern Christian Leadership Conference), Congressman from Georgia, U.S. Ambassador to United Nations, mayor of Atlanta

Young, Whitney M., Jr., Executive Director, National Urban League [1921-1971]

About people referred to in the quotes

PLEASE NOTE: The number in ( ) is the page where a name appears. Individuals already identified in THE VOICES listing are not included.

Carver, George Washington (88), world famous agricultural scientist, developed innovative farming techniques [c.1861-1943]

Gandhi, Mahatma (54), Indian leader, whose non-violent principles led to ridding his country of British rule in 1946, assassinated by a Hindu fanatic [1869-1948]

Jackson, Sam[uel] (91), film actor

Lee, Spike (91), actor/writer/director/producer

Louis, Joe (88), long-time heavyweight boxing champion, known as "the Brown Bomber" [1914-1981]

Marshall, Thurgood (91), NAACP attorney who won *Brown vs. Board of Education of Topeka*, first African-American Supreme Court Justice [1908-1993]

Poitier, Sidney (91), helped break the Hollywood stereotype of Negroes as inferior, first black Oscar winner, 1992 Lifetime Achievement Award

Quayle, Dan (67), Vice President under President George Bush, known for his verbal bloopers

Roddenberry, Gene (147), television producer, creator of Star Trek®, the first science fiction series to use an ethnically diversified cast [1921-1991]

Steinbeck, John (85), novelist, best known for his 1939 classic of the Depression, *The Grapes of Wrath* [1902-1968]

Till, Emmett (75), 14-year-old black Chicago boy, son of Mamie Mobley (see VOICES), brutally murdered in Mississippi in 1955 by relatives of a white woman he had spoken to without the "proper" respect for Southern womanhood

Tyson, Mike (71), boxing champion with a tendency toward notoriety

Washington, Denzel (91), versatile black actor who played Malcolm X in Spike Lee's film

Williams, Venus (89), black tennis prodigy

Woods, Tiger (89), golf prodigy, whose mother is Thai and whose father is African-American and Native-American

ABOUT THE EDITOR

Ella Mazel (B.A., Hunter College, 1938) is a long-time editor and book designer, sometime author, mother of four, grandmother of five.

Her article, "Conductor from Harlem: Dean Dixon Makes His Way With Baton Despite Many Hazards," was published in *The New York Times*, January 11, 1941. Many years and several careers later, in 1978, she had the privilege of designing, editing, and producing Philip S. Foner's *Paul Robeson Speaks: Writings, Speeches, Interviews*.

From 1967 to 1973 she compiled, and revised annually, a college guide used widely by high school guidance counselors and students. Originally called *Colleges at Your Fingertips*, it was eventually issued as *The New York Times Guide to College Selection*.

In 1995, she compiled, arranged and annotated, designed, and produced *Ahead of Her Time: A Sampler of the Life and Thought of Mary Wollstonecraft*, excerpts from the letters and writings of the great pioneer of the feminist movement.

The present volume is probably her swan song (famous last words), a labor of love that she hopes will make a difference.

Collect-your-own quotes

"If people just clipped the newspaper and analyzed the issues from a perspective of racial justice every day, their consciousness and their actions would change. They could no longer be mere observers of the daily inequality and cruel disdain manifested so boldly through our history and our current reality. Your book is an example of what people can do as a start on the problem."

MARILYN CLEMENT
Executive Director,The Women's International League for Peace and Freedom

This is an invitation to follow my example. It was hard for me to accept the fact that I could no longer include many items that appeared after I had finalized the book. The process is open ended. So I've left these pages for you to continue my work.

You'll be surprised how many news stories relating to racism turn up virtually every day if you're tuned in. Use these pages to copy or paste in whatever pithy quotes you come across in your reading. For complete articles, use a folder or a scrapbook.